MW00713998

#1 *NEW YORK TIMES* BESTSELLING AUTHOR

MIKE EVANS

FINDING GOD IN THE PLAGUE

TimeWorthy
B·O·O·K·S

P.O. Box 30000, Phoenix, AZ 85046

This book is lovingly dedicated to my dear friend,
Leonard Ravenhill (1907-1994)

Leonard Ravenhill was an English Christian
evangelist and author who greatly impacted my life.
I had the honor of visiting him in his home
just before he died. On the ceiling above his bed
he had written the word "eternity"
to remind him of focusing on heaven.
During our final meeting, he asked me
two questions that have challenged me to this day.
First, he asked, "Are the things
you're living for worth Christ dying for?"
Second, he asked, "Are you living your life
in the light of eternity, so you don't fear eternity?"
I pray this book honors his perspective and
leads you to better live for what is eternal.

CONTENTS

INTRODUCTION 7

CHAPTER 1
DID GOD SEND THE PLAGUE? 17

CHAPTER 2
GOD'S GLORY IN THE PLAGUE 33

CHAPTER 3
THE FIRST CHURCH OF BABYLON 47

CHAPTER 4
THE BABYLONIAN REBUKE 65

CHAPTER 5
THE POWER OF THE CROSS 77

CHAPTER 6
THE MYSTERY OF THE CROSS 97

CHAPTER 7
THE PROMISE OF THE SPIRIT PART 1:
A HEAVENLY POWER SURGE 111

CHAPTER 8
THE PROMISE OF THE SPIRIT PART 2:
WHEN HEAVEN INVADES EARTH 125

CHAPTER 9

THE IDOLS ARE COMING DOWN 137

CHAPTER 10

THE PLAGUE OF THE HEART 149

CHAPTER 11

THE THIRD GREAT AWAKENING...169

CHAPTER 12

IMITATION ALTARS...189

CHAPTER 13

I SAW THE LORD...201

CHAPTER 14

TAKE OFF YOUR CROWN 215

CHAPTER 15

A CALL TO PRAYER 233

CHAPTER 16

A GREAT AWAKENING OR A RUDE AWAKENING? 245

CHAPTER 17

TRUE REPENTANCE...255

INTRODUCTION

F*inding God in the Plague* was written during the plague of the coronavirus during my time of radical prayer and repentance before the Lord. I hope you discover what I saw in this revelation because it changed my life. One word from God can change your life forever.

Many ask me, "What is the key to your success?" I'm a number one *New York Times* bestselling author and have 105 published books that have been read by more than 43 million people. I've written over 5,000 articles and have met with over 70 world leaders. I am currently advising three world leaders. I'm also the founder of two beautiful museums, Friends of Zion in Jerusalem and the Corrie Ten Boom Museum in Haarlem, Holland.

As I complete the final words of this book, I've just returned from meeting with U.S. Secretary of State Mike Pompeo, and presented him with the Friends of Zion Award for his support of Israel and was briefed on the current situation in Israel. Over the last 48 hours, I've conducted 18 interviews with major Israeli and American media in support of Israel and the Jewish people.

I'm not saying all this to brag about myself; I'm saying it to brag on God. I know who I am. All the great things God has done in my life have come through dark times that in many ways were like a plague. My first plague happened when I was 11. My childhood was one of unspeakable terrors. My father began abusing me at the age of four because he believed my mother had had an affair for two years with a Jewish man, and that I was not his son.

The abuse was violent. He would strip me naked and beat me with extension cords and coat hangers. Because of the ongoing, violent abuse, I developed tremendous problems—a speech impediment, a stomach ulcer, and was crippled by numerous fears. I had a fear of the dark, of death, of heights, and a fear of people.

I did not believe in God or Jesus. My mother told me at a very young age that she named me after her grandfather, Rabbi Mikel Katznelson, who had been burned alive in a synagogue with 2,000 other Jews. I later found out that the ninth president of Israel, Shimon Peres, who was until his death the chairman of my Friends of Zion museum, also had a grandfather, rabbi cantor Zvi Meltzer, in that same synagogue. He was also burned to death.

My father claimed to be an evangelical Christian. He attended church every Sunday. He tithed. They called him Brother Bob. But he was a womanizer and a very mean drunk. He would often beat my mother when he came home on Friday nights between one and two in the morning.

He never called me son. He never said I love you. He never affirmed me. What happens to a little boy like that? I think you know. He often ends up in prison for life or becomes a drug addict or an alcoholic, or commits suicide. He certainly doesn't end up happily married for 50 years to his best friend with children and grandchildren who adore him.

But that's precisely what happened to me. I remember one Tuesday in school when the teacher asked us children, "What do you want to be when you grow up?" The teacher had told us on Monday to think about it. I was terrified, because my only goal was to become 20 years old. That may sound strange to you, but I was sure my father would kill me before then. He almost succeeded several times.

One time on my way home I found a jackknife in the snow. I was so proud of myself. I showed it to him. He called me a liar and said, "God hates liars. You stole it. If you found it in the snow it would have been rusty." He took me into the basement, stripped me naked, took an extension cord, and started beating me. He held onto one of my arms and beat me with the extension cord in his other hand, and screaming, "God hates liars! I will beat you to death if I have to, until you tell me truth."

He almost did beat me to death. He beat me until I was hysterical and wet myself. He beat me until I could hardly think. I was a bloody mess. I desperately tried to come up with a lie so that he would stop, but I was in such a state of shock that I could not.

I was 11 years old and had to show up for school on Tuesday and say what I wanted to be when I grew up. Everyone had their dreams, like being a pilot or doctor or an astronaut. I intentionally showed up late to school because I hoped the teacher wouldn't call on me. I sat in the last seat in the room, positioned near the red bell. I remember that bell, hoping it would ring so I could get out of there before the teacher called on me. Unfortunately, my plan did not work.

My teacher asked me, "Michael, what do you want to be when you grow up?"

Because I stuttered, I said, "I want to to-to be-be-be 20."

The teacher said, "What? I didn't understand you." I said it again. "You want to grow up to be 20?"

"Yes."

Everyone in the class looked at me and started laughing. Then the red bell rang. I ran out of that classroom crying, so embarrassed and humiliated, because that was truly my only goal, to be alive at 20. That was on a Tuesday.

That following Friday night, it looked as if that goal would never be achieved. Early Saturday morning, I woke up somewhere around

1:30 to the sound of my mother crying. I walked to the top of the stairs and spotted my father, forcing her to sit in a chair while he slapped her, calling her a Jewish whore, accusing her of having had an affair with a Jewish man, and shouting, "You know he's not my son. He's a bastard!"

I cried and felt so ashamed because I'd seen this scene many times, yet I was a coward. I was afraid to protect my mother. I was a skinny little guy and my father was a big, muscular man.

As I sat in agony crying, I had no faith. Because of what had happened to my great-grandfather, I didn't believe in God, and because my father claimed to believe in Jesus and said he was a good Christian, I didn't believe in Jesus. I thought it was all faked.

But as my mother was crying, something in me snapped. I screamed out in the dark, "Stop it!"

After I had screamed out, my father flew up those stairs like a raging bull. He reached out, grabbed me by the throat, and lifted me above his head. I reached out to grab his hands because I was in excruciating pain. I looked into those bloodshot eyes and realized I wasn't going to live to be 20. I was going to die that night.

The next thing I remember was waking up from an unconscious state, gagging. I was in a fetal position on the floor. I don't know how long I had been there. I had vomited all over myself, but I was alive. I was angry I had survived, because I saw no purpose for my life. This man hated me, and I believed my mother was suffering because of me. In the dark, in my personal plague, I shouted at God, screaming loudly, "God, why was I born?"

When I said that, I suddenly noticed a light coming toward me. It scared me. I thought it was my father coming back to finish me off. I lifted my hands to protect my face. The light grew brighter and brighter. It seemed like hours, but was probably only a few seconds of quiet.

I suddenly knew it couldn't be my father, because he would have been raging and cursing and screaming. I dared to peak through my fingers at the light. When I did, I saw something I had never seen before or since. I saw two hands reaching toward me. There were nail scars on His wrists. Could it be Jesus? I thought I must be out of my mind because I didn't even believe in Jesus.

I looked up a little higher and could then see His eyes. It was the first time I had ever seen a man with smiling eyes. They were the eyes of Jesus. Every color in the rainbow was in those eyes, blues and greens and every color. They were like magnets when I looked at them. I couldn't stop looking. They just drew me in.

He spoke as He looked at me, calling me, "Son." I had never heard the word son from my father. No one had ever called me son.

Then He said, "I love you."

I had never heard those words. I would say, "I love you," to my mother, but she had been abused so much she couldn't say them. She only said, "Me too."

Next, He said, "I have a great plan for your life." Then He suddenly left.

I cried the rest of that night, but in joy, because now I had hope. It was hope I had never experienced.

I realized in the morning that I didn't stutter anymore and that my stomach didn't hurt when I ate. I also noticed that I wasn't afraid anymore. I wasn't afraid of the dark, of people, of heights, or even death. I had been radically transformed by the grace of God, and I didn't even understand what any of it meant. I had come to glorious faith in a living Savior.

But what I also saw that morning were the lines from my father's fingers around my neck when I looked in the mirror. He had choked me so severely that blood came to the surface. Everywhere his fingers had been, you could see their prints around my neck.

At 11 years old, I had gone through my own personal plague, but it was the greatest day of my life. And yes, it was also the worst.

Since that day I've encountered many personal plagues. I know of at least a dozen occasions. Some of them have been in war zones such as Somalia with Al-Qaeda attempting to assassinate me. Another was in Cambodia with the Khmer Rouge trying to kill me. Still another time was in the Persian Gulf during the Iraq War when it looked like I was going to die. Yes, I have experienced many personal problems, but God has always shown up in my plagues. He revealed Himself beyond anything I could have comprehended.

I'm sharing this with you because I know how painful plagues are and how paralyzing fear can be. I want you to know the plague you've gone through includes a path to the presence and the power of God in a way that you've never experienced. I pray that the words in this book will help you look to the Lord during your plagues and that God will receive all the glory.

"THE PEOPLE
THAT DO KNOW
THEIR GOD
SHALL BE STRONG,
AND DO
EXPLOITS."

-DANIEL 11:32, KJV

DID GOD SEND
THE PLAGUE?

"Did God send the plague?" This is a question I've heard probably a hundred times from different people: Did He send this plague? If so why? People want answers. I'm not going to give you answers based on my opinion. That's completely irrelevant. Everyone else's opinion is irrelevant. The only thing that's relevant is what the Word of God says. Let's look at what the Bible teaches about plagues.

First, let's look at Jesus. He established the Lord's Supper. Yet the Lord's Supper was also a commemoration of a plague. The Passover was celebrated on the same night the Lord had passed over the Jewish people and struck all firstborn males of Egypt with death. The Lord's Supper also commemorates another plague, the death of Christ. It was all predicted in the Last Supper and even in the Psalms. The revelation of the Passover plague was that the angel of death could be stopped only by the blood of the Lamb.

Many say plagues are exclusive to the Old Testament. They would argue that we're New Testament believers, and that plagues no longer take place: "God doesn't send plagues today; we're under grace." I want you to look at three Scriptures in the Old Testament on this issue:

> "For at this time, I will send all my plagues to your very heart, and on your servants and on your people, that you may know that there is none like me in all the Earth" (Exodus 9:14).

> "But while the meat was still between their teeth, before it was chewed, the wrath of the Lord was aroused against the people, and the Lord struck the people with a very great plague" (Numbers 11:33).

> "If you do not carefully observe all the words of this law that are written in this book, that you may fear this glorious and awesome name, the Lord your God, then the Lord will bring upon you and your descendants

extraordinary plagues, great and prolonged plagues, and serious and prolonged sickness" (Deuteronomy 28:58-59).

This passage in Deuteronomy includes the last words of Moses before Joshua led the children of Israel into the Promised Land. God talked to him about the covenant people, the people of promise. He warned him that even though they were entering into the Promised Land, if they took their eyes off God and put idols between them and God, there would be consequences.

In Deuteronomy 28:61, we read, "Also, every sickness, every plague which is not written in the book of the law will the Lord bring upon you until you are destroyed. The Lord will bring upon you all the diseases and plagues." Again, the Lord is talking to His covenant people. Can you imagine that? This is Joshua, the leader who would be known for a victory in Jericho with the walls falling down, being warned by Moses, the man of God. He was told that plagues would come upon them if they disobeyed, and the Lord would send those plagues.

In 1 Samuel 5:7, the Ark of the Covenant had been taken into the land of the Philistines. God sent a plague so great that the idol Dagon fell on its face. What an illustration! "When the men of Ashdod saw how it was, they said, 'The Ark of God of Israel must not remain with us, for His hand is harsh towards us and our god.'" It's a great example of what happens when the church makes a covenant with the world.

I want you to look at these two Scriptures:

"And David built there an altar to the Lord and offered burnt offerings and peace offerings. So the Lord heeded the prayers for the land, and the plague was withdrawn from Israel" (2 Samuel 24:25).

"Behold, the Lord will strike your people with a serious affliction, your children, your wives, and all your possessions" (2 Chronicles 21:14).

In the first passage, the plague was stopped by David's obedience to the Lord. Plagues are a sign of God's wrath, usually regarding idolatry.

Yet many will insist, "That's the Old Testament, but I'm in the New Testament of God's grace. We don't have plagues now." Unfortunately, some of today's pastors give you smooth words of comfort while people are suffering because of plagues, and even dying.

When Jesus healed a blind man in John 5:14, He told him, "See, you have been made well. Sin no more, lest a worse thing come upon you." Do you see that? ". . .lest a worse thing come upon you."

We also read in Acts 5 about a story of two amazing church members, Ananias and Sapphira. They gave a large financial gift to the church, but they were not honest with their gift. They lied to the Holy Spirit, and both were suddenly struck dead.

Let's also look further in the New Testament at Revelation, also called the Apocalypse. The word "apocalypse" comes from the Greek word meaning an unveiling. We've been in a plague, but there will also be plagues in the future. If you read the book of Revelation, you'll see this on multiple occasions.

Revelation 9:18: "By these three *plagues* a third of mankind was killed—by the fire and the smoke and the brimstone which came out of their mouths."

Revelation 9:20: "But the rest of mankind who were not killed by these plagues did not repent of the works of their hands that they should not worship demons and idols of gold, silver, brass, stone, and wood, which can neither see nor hear nor walk."

The people would not repent. They hardened their hearts despite the plague. This is precisely what the late Pastor David Wilkerson told me in 1986. He preached that there is idolatry and unrepentance in the church, and a plague was coming because of it.

Revelation 11:6: "These have power to shut heaven, so that no rain falls in the days of their prophecy; and they have power over waters to turn them to blood, and to strike the earth with all plagues, as often as they desire."

These men will have the power to strike the world with plagues from God, just as Moses predicted to Joshua.

Revelation 15:1, "Then I saw another sign in heaven, great and marvelous: seven angels having the seven last plagues, for in them the wrath of God is complete."

Revelation 15:6-8, "And out of the temple came the seven angels having the seven plagues, clothed in pure bright linen, and having their chests girded with golden bands. Then one of the four living creatures gave to the seven angels seven golden bowls full of the wrath of God who lives forever and ever. The temple was filled with smoke from the glory of God and from His power, and no one was able to enter the temple till the seven plagues of the seven angels were completed."

Revelation 18:4, "And I heard another voice from heaven, saying, Come out of her, my people that ye may not be partakers of her sins and that ye receive not of her plagues."

Plagues continue to be mentioned in the final two chapters of Revelation that describe the new heaven and the new earth. Revelation 21:9 mentions seven angels with the last seven plagues: "Then one of the seven angels, who had seven bowls filled with seven plagues, came to me and talked with me saying, 'I will show you the bride, the lamb's wife.'"

Do you know what this is all about? It's talking about Jesus, the King of kings and the Lord of lords. It refers to our Savior. When did He come? In the midst of a plague! God cleanses through plagues. Don't take it lightly. Plagues are the judgment of God.

Plagues are sent to lead people to repent. We must humble ourselves. We must look at this issue from the Word of God. My opinion doesn't matter. Your pastor's opinion doesn't matter. Only the Word of God matters.

Look at the last words of the Book of Revelation. Last words are very important. Revelation 22:18 reads, "For I testify to everyone who hears the words of the prophecy of this book: If anyone adds to these things, God will add to him the plagues that are written in this book."

The Bible even ends with the warning to not change God's Word. Those who do so will experience plagues. If you are taking the Word of God and adding to it, or removing anything from it, you will experience plagues.

Some pastors are not preaching against sin. Do you know that the moral standard of the world is determined by the moral standard in the church? When pastors refuse to preach against sin, there's no conviction in the pews. They are taking away from the Word of God. When pastors refuse to preach against hell, they are taking away from the Word of God. When they're adding cheap grace and exemption from judgment, they are putting themselves and their congregation in a position to bring the plagues of God on their own heads. Yes, plagues are from God. This latest plague was surely allowed by God, and there will likely be plagues in the future.

Why are we experiencing plagues? What is the number one reason this plague has come upon humanity? It is because mankind shook its fist in the face of God and embraced secular humanism, not only in the world, but also in the church. Secular humanism is when man meets your needs, where your focus is on man, not on the Lord. But the Bible says, "The fear of the Lord leads to life" (Proverbs 18:23).

The Hebrew word for fear includes awe of the exalted, an overwhelming sense of His glory. The fear of God also implies the hatred of evil and wrong.

You don't hear a great deal of preaching against sin today. Why? Because of religious secular humanism. The Gospel is being radically influenced in the church by a secular humanistic world. Many say, "Look at how big our church is. Look at how prosperous our church is." Tell it to the first church of Sodom and Gomorrah!

Secular humanism puts man on the throne. It does not mind man worshipping God or claiming to know God, so long as man is on the throne.

Secular humanism promotes tolerance for immoral behavior.

Secular humanism rejects absolute moral standards.

You won't be convicted in a seeker-friendly church. You won't come into that church crying in repentance and falling on your face, because they're taking away from the Word of God, or they're adding to it. You can be sure of one thing: When the Antichrist takes control of this planet he'll take control of religion, because the spirit of the Antichrist is in many churches today.

How will he do that? He'll do it because the road has already been paved by seeker-friendly preachers, who will not preach on hell, will not preach on sin, and will leave sinners feeling comfortable. Many are familiar with the words of Solomon in 2 Chronicles 7:14, but few are familiar with verses 13-15:

> "When I shut up heaven and there is no rain, or I command the locusts to devour the land, or I send pestilence among My people, if My people which are called by my name humble themselves, and pray and seek My face,

and turn from their wicked ways, then I will hear from Heaven, I will forgive their sin and will heal their land. Now My eyes will be open and My ears attentive to their prayers in this place."

First, God sends plagues to humble us. Solomon affirms what we've studied throughout the Bible. God uses droughts and locusts and sickness and plagues to humble us, to help us realize that we're not in control. He shuts up the skies. Instead of feasting, we're living in fear. The preacher Andrew Murray wrote, "Pride must die in you, or nothing of heaven can live in you." Religious pride must die in us, or nothing of heaven can live in us.

Second, the response to the plague needs to be prayer and repentance. When we humble ourselves, it's a call to holiness. Evangelist D.L. Moody once said, "It is a great deal better to live a holy life than to talk about it." We are told to let our light shine, and if it does we won't need to tell anybody it does, the light will be our witness, our own witness. He adds, "Lighthouses don't ring bells and fire cannons to call attention to their shining. They just shine."

1 Peter 1:16 says, "Be holy, for I am holy." Peter referred to what God said in the Torah, the Law of Moses. Holiness comes at a cost. That cost is repentance and prayer and humility. The late evangelist Leonard Ravenhill noted, "The world has lost the power to blush over its vice. The church has lost her power to weep over it." When

was the last time you really repented before the Lord? When was the last time you cried out to God for forgiveness, and saw yourself the way He sees you? In Luke 18:10-14, Jesus rebuked the religious leaders of His time. He said to them:

> "Two men went up to the temple to pray, one was a Pharisee, the other was a tax collector. The Pharisee stood and prayed thus with himself, 'God, I thank You that I'm not like other men—I'm not unjust or an adulterer or a tax collector. I fast twice a week; I give tithes.' And the tax collector, standing afar off, would not so much as raise his eyebrows to heaven, but he beat his breast, saying, 'God, be merciful to me a sinner!' 'I tell you,' Jesus said, 'this man went down to his house justified rather than the other; for everyone who exalts himself will be humbled, and he who humbles himself will be exalted.'"

Yes, we have a problem right now in Christianity. Some Christian preachers and evangelists really believe they are celebrities. Some believe it so strongly that have their own private jets. They have a bodyguard. They may even call themselves influencers, but there are no celebrities at the foot of the cross. The only celebrity in the presence of a holy God is Jesus, the Lamb of God.

Our problem is that we tend to identify more with the Pharisee than the tax collector. Religion does that to us. We are to be more like the repentant tax collector, admitting our sins, humbling ourselves, crying out to God. If you can't cry out to God in the plague, your heart is as hard as stone.

Plagues pass when we respond to God's judgment. God does not send endless plagues with the desire to destroy us. He sends plagues with the desire to restore us. Look at all the positive aspects that follow a prayerful, repentant heart during a plague: "I will hear from heaven and forgive their sin and heal their land. My eyes will be open, my ears will be attentive to their prayer in this place" (2 Chronicles 7:14). When we pray and repent, God hears and responds.

Do you want the plague to pass? There's a path to ending the plague. In Nehemiah 9:2-3, the people of God had returned to Jerusalem after 70 years of bondage. They had disobeyed the Lord by marrying people who did not follow their God, but when called upon to repent, they did. Then those who repented separated themselves and confessed their sins. They stood up when they heard the reading of the Word of the Lord. The Bible says that they repented and confessed and worshipped the Lord.

The key is that they obeyed. They didn't continue in sin. They separated themselves from their sinful ways. If we want the plague to pass, we must truly change from our sins and do what is right. They confessed. They both did what was right and confessed what was wrong. Sometimes we try to change the past without confessing. But in this case, the people publicly announced their wrongdoings.

When was the last time you heard sinners crying out in repentance? When was the last time you saw a pastor crying out from the pulpit in repentance? The Word says that if we confess our sins, He's faithful and just to forgive us of those sins (1 John 1:9).

A sign of authentic confession is true brokenness. In the classic book *The Calvary Road* written by British evangelist Roy Hession we find, "This is ever the nature of true confession of sin, true brokenness. It is the confession that my sin is not just a mistake, a slip, or something which is really foreign to my heart ('Not really like me to have such thoughts or do such things!'), but it is something which reveals the real 'I'; that shows me to be proud, rotten, the unclean thing God says that I am. . ."

David confessed his sins. He humbled himself and he was a king. He wasn't trying to justify himself by gathering people to tell him how wonderful he was. He humbled himself in the presence of God (Psalm 51:4).

The second thing that happened in the midst of a plague is that they listened. I love this thought! The people had gathered for a time of revival, listening to the Word of God being read for one-fourth of each day. We're talking about three or four hours at a time! They wanted to be in the Word. We have more access to the Bible today than at any time in history, yet many of us rarely read God's Word for ourselves. For many of us, God's Word is not transforming our lives. We have one foot in the world and the other in the temple. It won't work.

Another thing that happened out of the Israelites experiencing the plague is that they worshipped. They concluded their time of repentance with adoration. Do you realize that a plague can end in praise? Maybe you need to stop watching TV or the news and start worshipping God, and repent and humble yourself. There's something about singing of our love to God that builds our faith in Him.

James 5:13 says, "Is anyone cheerful? Let him sing psalms." If you don't know where to begin, turn to the middle of your Bible and find God's source of joy in the Psalms. A plague brings us to our knees, but it's not intended to leave us in despair. Through repentance, we can rejoice with our hands in the air.

I'm seeing a fire, and I'm seeing a plague. I'm seeing three Jews in a furnace, men who refused to bend or bow or burn. And I'm seeing a king who says, "There's a fourth man in the midst of the furnace, and he looks like the son of God." Hallelujah! God is coming in the midst of this plague. God sends plagues. He did in the past. He's doing it now. He'll do it in the future. But they're only to turn our hearts to Him and to pursue holiness.

Today we've forgotten what the word holiness means. We think it means happiness. On March 10, 1998, David Wilkerson preached a message entitled "The Dangers of the Gospel of Accommodation."

His words stirred my heart as I sought the Lord in repentance during the COVID-19 crisis. He stated, "The Gospel of Jesus Christ is one of self-denial. Jesus said, 'If any man will come after me, let him deny himself, take up his cross and follow Me.'"

Self-denial is not something you give; it's something you give up. The giving up of yourself, giving up everything you are. It's a living sacrifice to the Lord Jesus Christ to present your body as a holy sacrifice acceptable to God, which is your reasonable service. God has every right to say to His church, "If you expect to give Me your resurrected body all through eternity, I have every right to ask you to devote your body to Me in this life. I want every part of you. Surrender to Me."

We're not here for our own pleasure and prosperity. We're here for the pleasure of the King. When we want His attention, when we focus on Him in the midst of a plague, His glory will come on us. A plague is painful, but it's also purposeful. Let us not forget the reason God sends plagues upon the land. Let us respond with a heart of confession and repentance and holiness before the Lord, in humility.

I realize this is a strong message, but it's not as strong as theologian Jonathan Edwards' message, "Sinners in the Hands of an Angry God" that birthed the First Great Awakening in the 1730s and '40s. God is calling us to fall on our faces and acknowledge that He sent the plague in order for us to repent. If we do, we'll hear from heaven in a way we've never experienced.

QUESTIONS FOR DISCUSSION

✧ How have the plagues of our time changed your life?

✧ What responses do you feel God is calling you to make as you face challenging times?

✧ In what ways do you need to change how you pray to respond to God during this time of plague?

✧ Who has God placed in your life who also needs to hear the message of God at work through plagues? How can you share this message of repentance and hope with them?

GOD'S GLORY

IN THE PLAGUE

"Arise, shine, for your light has come, and the glory of the Lord rises upon you. See, darkness covers the earth and thick darkness is over the peoples, but the Lord rises upon you, and His glory appears over you. Nations will come to your light, and kings to the brightness of your dawn. Lift up your eyes and look about you: All assemble and come to you; your sons come from afar, and your daughters are carried on the hip. Then you will look and be radiant, your heart will throb and swell with joy; the wealth of the seas will be brought to you, to you the riches of the nations will come. Herds of camels will cover your land, young camels of Midian and Ephah. And all from Sheba will come, bearing gold and incense and proclaiming the praise of the Lord. The sun will no more be your light by day, nor will the brightness of the moon shine on you, for the Lord will be your everlasting light, and your God will be your glory. Your sun will never set again, and your move will way no more; the Lord will be your everlasting light and your days of sorrow will end." (Isaiah 60:1-6; 19–20)

Aren't these words amazing? The days of sorrow are ended. God will be your glory in the midst of deep darkness.

President Donald Trump referred to the coronavirus as a plague. He's correct. Other leaders are saying the same thing. Let's talk about plagues throughout history. COVID-19 certainly wasn't the first plague.

What is a plague? A plague is usually defined as an infectious disease. For example, the Bubonic plague killed millions of people from 541 to 542. The 1918 Spanish Flu was the most severe plague in American history. Between 1918 and 1919, about 500 million people, or one third of the world's population at that time, became infected with this virus. The number of deaths was estimated to be at least 50 million worldwide, with about 675,000 occurring in the United States.

When we look at the Scriptures, Moses saw God's hand at work in a time of testing and plague. God always has a plan during our problems. God whispers to us in our pleasures, but shouts in our pain. Pain is God's megaphone to rouse a deaf church and a deaf world.

God wants to reveal Himself regarding how great He is during difficult times. The Lord said to Moses: "I will bring one more plague on Pharaoh and on Egypt. And afterward he will let you go. When he lets you go, he will surely drive you out of here altogether" (Exodus 11:1). The children of Israel were moving from bondage into freedom, out of despair into hope, and out of obscurity into prominence. That's what a plague can do. After their deliverance, they rejoiced with great joy.

Exodus 15:1-2 notes, "Then Moses and the children of Israel sang this song to the Lord, and spoke, saying: 'I will sing to the Lord, for He has triumphed gloriously! The horse and its rider He has thrown into the sea! The Lord is my strength and song. And He has become my salvation; He is my God and I will praise Him; My father's God, and I will exalt Him.'" What they viewed as painful, Moses viewed as critical to their destiny. God sent them in so that He could bring them out.

Their liberation included 10 plagues. The final plague resulted in the death of the firstborn sons of the land. It was only after these 10 plagues that God's people experienced deliverance. We all want deliverance and freedom, but no one wants a plague. Yet God often works through difficult situations like plagues to fulfill His purpose in our lives.

In the previous chapter, we were given the key Scriptures regarding God's work through plagues. In the case of Moses and God's people, the plagues they experienced prepared them for their divine destiny. However, to achieve God's plan, both Moses and the people of God first had to endure a time of quarantine, a time of sheltering, during which God prepared his heart, and the hearts of the children of Israel for the coming plague.

God works through our times of shelter. Corrie Ten Boom was a person I came to know well. We purchased and restored her home as a museum to tell the story of her bestselling book *The Hiding Place*. She talked about being locked up in solitary during the Holocaust. She told me she was lifted up while she was locked up.

Those who had been humiliated were now honored: "And the Lord gave the people favor in the sight of the Egyptians. Moreover the man Moses was very great in the land of Egypt. In the sight of Pharaoh's servants, and in the sight of his people" (Exodus 11:2–3).

Those who had been afraid were now feared: "But against none of the children of Israel shall a dog move its tongue, against any man or beast, that you may know that the Lord does make a difference between the Egyptians and Israel" (Exodus 11:7).

Those who had been rejected were now sought after: "A mixed multitude went up with them also, with their flocks and their herds—a great deal of livestock" (Exodus 12:38).

God does some of his best work through our times of shelter. What happened to Noah after God sheltered him and his family for a year in the ark? He came out and became the father of many nations.

What happened to David after he was anointed king and was sheltered for 15 years, including hiding in a cave in Ein Gedi? He became the king of Israel, a man after God's own heart, and was in the genealogy of Jesus Christ. Jesus is not called the son of Abraham or the son of Jacob, but the son of David.

What happened to Elijah after God sheltered him by the brook? He traveled to Mount Carmel and called the glory and the power of God down against the prophets of Baal.

What happened to Daniel when he was sheltered in a lions' den? God rescued him and closed the mouths of the lions.

What happened to Jonah after he was sheltered in the belly of a great fish? His preaching shook Nineveh. The people repented and there was a mighty revival.

What happened to John the Baptist after being sheltered in the wilderness? He proclaimed the word of the Lord and baptized Jesus Christ.

What happened to Paul after he had spent three years sheltered in the wilderness after his conversion? He came back and turned the world upside down.

What happened to John the Apostle after he was sheltered on the island of Patmos in a cave? Jesus appeared to him with a vision that today is called the Book of Revelation.

Best of all: What happened to Jesus after he had been sheltered in the tomb for three days? He came out and brought salvation to the world! God works through our times of shelter. When God shelters us, He's preparing us.

We see this in the life of Moses. He spent 40 years in the desert, tending sheep after being a prince of Egypt. Yet God was preparing him for sanctification, and for the fire that he would experience. He called out to God in that fire, *"Hineni!"* In Hebrew, it means, "You see through me." Oh, that we would say today, "God, You see through me."

Moses said, "I'm no longer a prince of Egypt." He said, "I can't even speak," but God made him into a prophet who transformed the world. When we reach that place, and see the fire of God burning, and the glory of God, we'll feel so unclean. We'll humble ourselves and we'll repent. We'll cry out, *"Hineni,"* You see through me. Abraham cried out similar words.

The prophet Isaiah also cried out in deep grief over the death of the king. Then he saw the glory of God appear and the Lord asked, "Whom shall I send and who will go for us?"

Isaiah answered, "Here am I, Lord. Send me!" (Isaiah 6:8).

That's what God is doing through this plague. He wants every minister to cry out, *"Hineni!"* He wants every member of every church to cry out, *"Hineni!"*

Let me give you some examples of God in a plague, during a crisis, with death all around, the smell of death, and the cry of death. The Israelites were in a shelter on the night of the first Passover. Everyone was sheltered.

Let's focus on that beautiful shelter. It was the blood of the lamb that made the difference. When you're sheltered, and when you've been in the presence of God, you'll cry out. You will see the power of the blood.

Everyone will ultimately face a plague. Death is a plague. We will all face that plague, but we won't face it alone, because there's Someone who conquered it and destroyed the sting of that plague.

When the plague struck Egypt, Moses was not the only one who experienced shelter. There was one plague where all the people of God were shut up in their homes. In Exodus 12 we read what took place on this eventful night. God predicted the judgment of death on firstborn sons. The only escape would be staying in your home and following God's instructions. What were his instructions? The people were required to place the blood of a lamb on the sides and top of their doorposts, remaining inside until the Lord passed over.

God humbled Moses so Moses could see how big God was, not how big the plague was. When you see a big God, you see a small plague. There was the smell of death and the cry of death. While the children of Israel were sheltered, they were focused on just one thing: the blood of the lamb.

In Exodus 12:5–8, it says the lamb was without blemish. The lamb was set apart. The lamb was sacrificed. The blood of the lamb was used to rescue them from the plague. Does this sound like any other lamb we find in the Bible?

The Lamb of God, Jesus Christ, was spotless and without sin.

The Lamb of God was set apart.

The Lamb of God was sacrificed for our sins.

The Lamb of God poured out His blood to rescue us from death.

His name is Jesus. This is the Lamb of God, who continues to rescue us today in our plague. But notice the order of this story as God worked in the Passover. The sheltering took place first, then the miracles. God shelters His people. It's God's promise for us today as well. God is sheltering us to save us, to work through us, and to drive us to prayer and repentance.

What happened after the Passover? The people experienced freedom and deliverance. Yet God's miracles did not end. The New Testament shows us that no matter how low we feel right now God is not done with us yet. When Jesus died, His followers hid. They sheltered in place in Jerusalem for three days before experiencing the resurrected power of Jesus.

For how long did Jesus return? He appeared for 40 days, like the 40 years God's people experienced in the wilderness before God fulfilled His promises. But after those 40 days, Jesus returned to the Father and His followers were told to wait in Jerusalem. Why were they to wait? God would send the Holy Spirit to make them witnesses in Jerusalem, Judea and Samaria, and to the ends of the earth (Acts 1:8).

I believe God is already preparing us for such a time. This time of quarantine, of being sheltered in, is drawing us to our knees in repentance to focus on only one thing—Jesus. I can tell you, out of this will come a manifestation of His glory like America and the world have never seen.

There's another thing that happens in a plague. God closed their doors so He could open their destiny. They were transformed from being the slaves of Egypt to becoming the army of Israel: "So you shall observe the Feast of Unleavened Bread, for on this same day I will have brought your armies out of the land of Egypt. Therefore you shall observe this day throughout your generations as an everlasting ordinance" (Exodus 12:17).

In the plague, they also changed from being outcasts to becoming overcomers:

> "It will come to pass when you come to the land which the Lord will give you, just as He promised, that you shall keep this service. And it shall be, when your children say to you, 'What do you mean by this service?' that you will say, 'It is the Passover sacrifice of the Lord, who passed over the houses of the children of Israel in Egypt when He struck the Egyptians and delivered our households.' So the people bowed their heads and worshiped" (Exodus 12:5–27).

Yet another thing that happens through a plague is that you're brought out to be brought in. Look at Deuteronomy 6:21-23:

> ". . .then you shall say to your son: We were slaves of Pharaoh in Egypt, and the Lord brought us out of Egypt with a mighty hand; and the Lord showed signs and wonders before our eyes, great and severe, against

Egypt, Pharaoh, and his household. Then He brought us out from there, that He might bring us in, to give us the land of which He swore to our fathers."

What are you seeing in this plague? Are you viewing things through the eyes of the Holy Spirit, focused on an eternal perspective? Or are you living in fear? Is the plague paralyzing you? It doesn't need to be. God has grace for you in this storm.

There is much more that happened in the plague with Moses:

The people saw restriction; Moses saw release.

The people saw sacrifice; Moses saw salvation.

The people saw loss and disruption; Moses saw gain.

The people saw trouble; Moses saw triumph.

Suffering can refine us rather than destroy us, because God Himself walks with us in the fire. God has used this time to show me His power and glory as I've humbled myself and repented and sought His face, and He'll do it for you.

You can accomplish more in one moment in His presence than in your entire lifetime out of it. God wants you to be part of another Great Awakening. He's going to bring it to this generation. It's going to come. You can either be part of it or you can miss out. The light is going to be brighter than the darkness. The glory of God is going to touch this nation and shake it and extend far beyond its borders to shake the world.

We don't hide from God in a plague; we live for God in a plague. Our goal is not to shrink back in a plague, but to hear Him say, "Well done, my good and faithful servant." When we were forced to shut down our museum in Jerusalem, my ministry heard from heaven and God reminded me that we have the most popular museum in the nation called Friends of Zion. The Lord said, "Make it a comfort center." We turned it into a distribution center to feed Holocaust survivors. We're doing that now, all over the nation. There are opportunities in plagues to be salt and light and to bring healing to broken hearts.

The Spirit of God is not in quarantine. The Spirit will strengthen you to conquer sin and to live victoriously in Christ.

God's Word is not in quarantine. The Word of God is not chained; it's living and active and sharper than any two-edged sword (Hebrews 4:12). We must be led by the Spirit, guided by the Word of God, on fire for the Lord, doing the will of God. A plague can be a path to God's purpose for you, for your community, and for your world as we serve God in this mighty Great Awakening that is coming.

It's a difficult thing to talk with you about a plague and tell you that it's God's judgment, but it is. 62 million babies have been aborted in America. Many in our nation are consumed with alcoholism, drug addiction, pornography, and other vices.

Billy Graham said, "If God doesn't judge America, he's going to have to repent to Sodom and Gomorrah." The plague is the judgment of God. But out of it, can also come the glory of God. As Isaiah said, "Darkness shall cover the earth, and deep darkness his people; but the Lord shall arise upon you, and His glory shall be seen in you" (Isaiah 60:2)

QUESTIONS FOR DISCUSSION

✧ What are some ways you see God bringing glory to Himself through the struggles our world is currently facing?

✧ Think of a time the Lord worked through a difficulty in your life to result in a blessing. How could He do something similar in your life during this time?

✧ The Israelites were required to obey God at the Passover before escaping after the plague. What are some ways God is calling you to obey Him during this time?

✧ Why do many fail to turn to God during times of plague or struggle? How can you help share the message of God's glory during a plague with someone?

THE FIRST CHURCH
OF BABYLON IN THE PLAGUE

The spirit of Babylon may be in your church, and you don't even know it! It's like a plague. It has an extraordinary capacity to cover itself in religious appearances that seem to be approved by God. It's very enticing, as it appeals to your flesh. Babylon has a way of doing that.

Revelation 18:4 says, "And I heard another voice from heaven saying, 'Come out of her, my people, lest you share in her sins, and lest you receive of her plagues.'"

Before we consider these words from the Book of Revelation, let's look back at Daniel in Babylon. Daniel was a man of God. He was in Babylon, but Babylon was not in him. The reason he was in Babylon was because of Israel's sins. There was captivity, judgment, and exile. The Jewish people had been taken away from the land of promise in Israel far away to Babylon.

Though the Jewish people were not slaves in Babylon, they were living in forced exile. When the people of God were taken away from the promise of God and the covenant land God had given them, and from the temple destroyed by Nebuchadnezzar, they weren't in slavery. Instead, they lived in exile. The slavery of the Jewish people in Egypt and their exile in Babylon were much different.

But Solomon, who built the temple in Jerusalem, fell into idolatry. He began to compromise with the world's system, and in the end, the result was that Nebuchadnezzar invaded and carried them into captivity. They were no longer living under the promises of God. They were living in a worldly system. They were no longer living as a holy people with the reverent fear of God.

There was an integration of the people of God with the system of the world. It was called Babylon. Yet Babylon was rebuked by God.

There was a king named Cyrus whom God used despite himself. The Lord delivered the Jewish people from Babylon, and from being destroyed. They were allowed to return to the Promised Land.

But how many went back? There were a quarter of a million Jews in Babylon, but only about 42,000 returned to Jerusalem. Why? They had become comfortable in Babylon. They weren't worshipping God there. They had a form of godliness. Everything seemed just fine.

They weren't interested in going anywhere. They were prospering. Everything was lovely, but not in God's eyes. Look at these biblical passages:

"Go forth from Babylon! Flee from the Chaldeans! With a voice of singing, declare, proclaim this, utter it to the end of the earth; say, 'The Lord has redeemed his servant Jacob!'" (Isaiah 48:20).

"In those days and in that time, says the Lord, the children of Israel shall come, they and the Children of Judah together; with continual weeping they shall come, and seek the Lord their God. They shall ask the way to Zion, with their faces toward it, saying, 'Come and let us join ourselves to the Lord in a perpetual covenant that will not be forgotten.' Move from the midst of Babylon, go out of the land of the Chaldeans; and be like the Rams before the flocks" (Jeremiah 50:4–5, 8).

"Flee from the midst of Babylon, and every one save his life! Do not be cut off in her iniquity, for this is the time of the Lord's vengeance; he shall recompense her" (Jeremiah 51:6).

These are powerful words! God sent the plague because of idolatry. I believe that just as Babylon was shaken, COVID-19 is shaking America and the world, trying to free us from Babylon. God wants Babylon out of us and us out of our Babylon! He's going to shake us until it happens. It's a refining fire.

God is saying to you, preachers, that it's time to put aside your fundraising projects and repent. It's time to seek God for a pure move of the Holy Spirit in your churches, through fasting and prayer and repentance. Otherwise, He will spew you out of His mouth, just as He rebuked five of the seven churches of Revelation.

A preacher recently met with his staff and told them, "I want to start a big fundraising campaign. We don't really need the money; I'm going to do it just to disciple the people." His goal was purely to build a flow of cash for the benefit of those leading the congregation. That's the spirit of Babylon in the church.

Look around. Christ is going to come soon. Where are the prophets warning the people to repent, instead of comforting them with smooth words? Too many are comforting the wicked in their iniquity.

Many years ago, I was invited to the birthday party of a billionaire. His name is Cullen Davis. At the time, his personal net worth was over $1 billion and his corporate net worth was over $2 billion. There were many well-known leaders there. In the middle of the birthday party, Cullen looked at me and said, "Mike Evans, do you have a word from God for me? Share it right now."

I did get a word from God, but I wasn't going to reveal it, because it was not something he would want his guests to hear. Instead, I avoided him.

A few minutes later he repeated, "Mike, I believe you have a word from God for me for my birthday. I want you to share it." I again avoided him.

The third time he said, "Everybody, stop. I want Mike Evans to come up here and give the word of the Lord that God has given him for my birthday."

I looked at him. This man had accepted Christ and was giving away large amounts of money. A lot of the people in the room had been recipients of his gifts. Three times he tried to give me money, but God said not to take it. I looked at him and said, "Thus saith the Lord, everything that you have is going to be taken from you by God Almighty, except your health and your soul."

Those were the hardest words I have ever spoken at a birthday party. Come to think of it, he never invited me back to another birthday party!

But within 12 months, it began. Everything he had was taken, except his health and his soul. He later told me, "Mike, you gave me a pure word." I can tell you, there were preachers there who rebuked me for what I said. They told me there was no truth coming out of my mouth.

Even in the plague, the prayer closets are empty. Even in the plague, tears of repentance are missing. That's the seduction of Babylon. As people play with their toys, preoccupying God's people with ease and prosperity and pleasure, God is calling us out from a carnal world, from careless living, to seek the Lord and to seek holiness.

Look around at what you're obsessed with. Is it the beach or movies or sports or entertainment? Or maybe just going to church? Where were the prophets to warn you of the coming plague? Those pillow prophets had nothing to say. They didn't warn you of the impending calamity, in the same way they didn't warn people in the time of Noah.

But just getting out of Babylon is not enough. It's not enough to say, "God has cleansed me, and I've left my old ways. I'm changed. I'm out of Babylon. I'm out of the religious graveyard." The Lord wants to shake Babylon out of our churches, bringing us back to the place of a sovereign move of the Holy Ghost and repentance.

He wants us to no longer amalgamate our churches with a Babylonian system. He desires for the people of God to passionately repent and pray and seek His face. Listen to these words from Jeremiah 6:14: "They have also healed the hurt of my people slightly, saying, 'Peace, peace!' When there is no peace."

Did you catch that? The Word says "slightly." That means lightly or lacking in substance. God's purge will do away with all silly, surface-gospel preaching that has no substance. God's bringing back a two-edged sword. He's bringing back men who have heard His command and cry out, "Thus saith the Lord!" The days of winking at sin are over. God demands holiness.

Do you know, what's interesting? When Israel was taken into captivity, they were a distinct people, but the spirit of Babylon changed them. I love the church, but I can tell you as a minister of the gospel for over 50 years, I think there's a lot of Babylon in the church. The church has been to Babylon a lot.

Tithing has become more sacred to many churches than the cross. It has become a golden calf. We must return to the cross. You say, "Why? We are there. I was saved at the cross."

There's more to the cross than salvation. Taking up His cross includes sanctification. It means being convicted when you go to an R-rated movie and there's profanity, using the Lord's name in vain, and with sexually explicit content. It means holiness. John's prophecy from Revelation is being fulfilled in many ways before our eyes. God is soon going to bring down every Babylonian church, every Babylonian ministry, and every lukewarm believer. A plague will do that.

By the way, who preaches to the preachers? I have a word from the Lord for you, Pastor. Some of you mega-pastors are worshiping golden calves. You say, "No way." Oh, yes! You won't preach against sin. You won't preach on repentance. There are no prayer meetings in your church. There are no messages on hell or the Second Coming, because the plague of Babylon is in your heart. Repent! While you refuse to speak on these truths, you condemn to hell every soul who does not tithe in your church.

I want to share a heartbreaking story with you. I once led a precious lady to Christ who was a hairdresser and cutting my hair. She had stage IV cancer. When she found the Lord, I sent her to a church. That was a big mistake on my part, because that precious lady, a brand-new believer, walked into a church where the pastor was screaming at the congregation. He was shouting, "If you don't tithe, you are cursed by God and are a thief!" She walked out of the church, turned her back on God, and died shortly thereafter.

God's preparing to do a new thing. He's going to bring down the proud, the famous, and the ambitious. He's lifting up the humble and the unknown, and bringing the church to repentance and holiness! It a move of God toward pastors who no longer live like celebrities. The day of superstar Christians is over.

There are not going to be any one-man shows in the next Great Awakening. There will be no one stealing God's glory and honor. No more showmanship and fog machines, or clever dramas, or world-class choreography. There will be no more big-time religion with unsaved consultants directing the church.

The Holy Ghost is going to shut down that commercial religion. He's not going to finance the ego of any preacher of the gospel. The plague is God's refining fire to purify the true saints. The Holy Spirit is already wooing the children of the Lord back from sensationalism. Even sinners are fed up with the manipulation. A revived, sanctified people will discern between the clean and the unclean.

When I first began serving in the ministry, Carolyn and I didn't have much. We were preaching at one place, and a doctor was so moved by my message that he told me, "I want to take you and your wife with my wife and me on a vacation."

We were shocked. We had never been on a vacation. We didn't have the money for vacations. When we got married, we went from Dallas to Oklahoma City for our honeymoon because we had no money.

This doctor took us to the beautiful Virgin Islands over the Christmas season with his wife and his children. He did it the next year and again the following year. It was amazing. He was a very wealthy man. He had a beautiful boat there, and even had an airplane.

One morning, I was praying in my room there and the Holy Ghost came upon me and said, "Go out and tell him this."

I walked out to that man and told him, "Thus saith the Lord: You're in sin. You're committing adultery with your secretary and you're cheating on your taxes. Within 36 months Satan is coming for you. If you don't repent, you'll get terminal cancer. It will begin in your stomach, it will spread through your organs, and you will die. Repent!"

Do you know what he did? He looked up at me and said, "You're 100 percent right. I am having an affair. I am cheating the government. But I'm not going to repent, because I have lots of Christian friends who are doing the same thing, and they're getting away with it."

I said, "We're leaving today, and I'll never see you again unless you repent." Thirty months later, his wife called me and said, "Would you come to the hospital? My husband has a stomach ulcer."

I said, "No, it's not a stomach ulcer; it is cancer and he's going to die."

I traveled to the hospital. He wanted to know if it was too late. I said, "It's too late. Your soul is going to be saved, but you're going to die." It broke my heart to say this to that dear man. But how could his heart be so hard that he looked at others in immorality and had no sense of guilt or shame? God is going to bring judgment upon our lives if we seek our own glory, if we seek to be comfortable and waste our time glorifying flesh and possessions rather than seeking the face of God.

God showed me that in the next Great Awakening, floods of people will come early to the front of churches, fall flat on their faces in the front of the altars, praying and repenting because God says, "My house will be a house of prayer." Listen to these words from Jeremiah 51:25-26:

"For see, I am against you, O mighty mountain, Babylon, destroyer of the earth! I will lift my hand against you, roll you down from your heights, and leave you, a burnt-out mountain. You shall be desolate forever; even your stones shall never be used for building again. You shall be completely wiped out."

Do you see that? In some ways, we have become exiled from our distinctiveness and we don't even realize it. We are not even a small glimmer of light to the world. Demons don't tremble anymore. Like Solomon, we have beautiful temples covered with gold. We are the envy of the world. We may have a church with marvelous music and messages, but we don't even comprehend that the spirit of Babylon is in that church.

The truth is that bit by bit, we've made a covenant with Babylon and don't even know it, just like the Jews did in Babylon. Babylon represents a backslidden, wicked society in collusion with an apostate world. It's a life of spiritual indifference, worldly compromise, and religious comfort, but with no holiness, no repentance, and no hell.

Yet even in the plague there's also a remnant. The remnant will be separated, a people whose hearts are stirred by the message of the Holy Spirit. These believers will no longer put up with wickedness and compromise in the church. They've heard the Holy Spirit calling them to a life of holiness and separation and repentance from the world. They have come out from Babylon, out from deadness and corruption and apostasy. They will no longer bow to the idols of this age. They are holy people, truly separated, a people hungry to go deeper in the Lord.

God is going to humble every minister who has false values, who chases after a world system. Jeremiah said, "The priests did not say, 'Where is the Lord?' and those who handle the law did not know me. The rulers also transgressed against me. The prophets prophesied by Baal, and walked after things that do not profit" (Jeremiah 2:8).

Jeremiah 10:21 added, "For the shepherds have become dull-hearted, and have not sought the Lord; therefore they shall not prosper, and all their flocks shall be scattered." These corrupt preachers don't see miracles in the church, or moves of the Holy Spirit. There are no divine interruptions, because they're smooth. They have it all figured out. But one thing they haven't figured out is how they're going to stand before a holy God in the midst of the plague, when he's putting the axe to the root and demanding repentance and holiness and intercession. God is calling his people out of Babylon. Jeremiah adds:

> "For the Lord, the God of Israel, says Babylon is like the wheat upon a threshing floor, in just a little while the flailing will begin" (Jeremiah 51:33).

"Move from the midst of Babylon, go out of the land of
the Chaldeans; and be like the rams before the flocks"
(Jeremiah 50:8).

Babylon continued to carry the people of God away in chains.
Paul reminds us that these things serve as an example and shadow of
spiritual things (Hebrews 8:5). Babylon is still the spirit of the world.
In this plague, we must come out of Babylon.

We're living in the age where the small churches are trying
to copy the big ones. Why? The big ones have defined success by
numbers and cash flow. Yet the truth is that some of these churches
have constructed walls to keep the Holy Ghost out so that there are
no interruptions. They say they're Spirit-filled, but there's no evi-
dence to prove it. The Holy Spirit could disappear and no one would
even notice.

As King Solomon allowed idolatry to spread throughout the
kingdom, the Spirit of God cried out, "Repent!" I want you to look at
1 Chronicles 17:1-5 and 2 Chronicles 1:6:

"Now it came to pass. This is the first temple that he's
speaking of. It came to pass when David was dwelling
in his house that David said to Nathan the prophet, 'See
now I dwell in a house of cedar, but the Ark of the Covenant of the Lord is under tent curtains.' Then Nathan

said to David, 'Do all that is in your heart for God is with you.' But it happened that night that the word of God came to Nathan saying, 'Go and tell my servant David thus says the Lord, you shall not build me a house to dwell in for I have not dwelt in a house since the time I brought up Israel, even to this day, but I have gone from tent to tent, from one tabernacle to another, wherever I have moved about with all Israel'" (1 Chronicles 17:1-5).

"And Solomon went up there to the bronze altar before the Lord, which was at the tabernacle of meeting, and offered a thousand burnt offerings on it" (2 Chronicles 1:6).

When man tries to build God a house, he tends to focus on how it looks. God is looking for a house where He dwells in your heart. He wants it to be clean and holy and passionate for Him. When the Israelites decided they wanted a king, and the prophet Samuel went to anoint the king, he was sent to the sons of Jesse.

Samuel expected God to choose the son who appeared the most likely candidate on the outside. Instead, God chose the rejected son and anointed him. He didn't choose the most popular person. He didn't choose the most likely person, instead God chose the least likely person. We know him as King David, a man after God's own

FINDING GOD IN THE PLAGUE

heart. There's something to be said about that. God's going to take people who are not in the spotlight and use them in a mighty way in this next Great Awakening.

Prior to the exile of the Jews from Jerusalem, man tried to build God a house. But God wanted a temple of purpose, not of appearance. He did not seek a man establishing his own ministry or kingdom. Jesus once told me during my time of prayer, "I've seen your ministry. Now I'm going to show you mine." That's entirely different.

Ezra 3:10 says, "When the builders laid the foundation of the temple of the Lord, the priests stood in their apparel with trumpets, and the Levites, the sons of Asaph, with cymbals, to praise the Lord, according to the ordinance of David king of Israel." The word of the Lord came to Ezra for Zerubbabel. He told him it was not by might, nor by power, but by my Spirit, says the Lord of hosts (also Zechariah 4:6). Zerubbabel was born in Babylon and was sent back to become the governor of Judea. What Zerubbabel was building was more about what you could see with your eyes than what was really inside it.

God desperately wants to detach us from physical appearances and move us into eternal purposes. When I was called to the ministry, I attended a seminary. I'll never forget being in a preaching class and a professor asked me, "What do you think of church?"

I said, "I hate it."

"What?" the professor exclaimed. "You're a minister, you have to like church."

I said, "I don't."

He said, "Why not?"

I said, "I don't know what it's for. If it's for preaching, I can go buy the sermon. There are great messages and books. If it's for singing, I can buy the music. What's the purpose of it? If it's just for fellowship, I can fellowship with people and go fishing. What's the purpose?"

He said, "You need to go back to your room and pray." I went back to my room and prayed, and God showed me that the purpose of the church is where my mind and my spirit ignite. That blew my mind. Now I love the church! Matthew 24:37–39 shares:

> "But as the days of Noah were, so also will the coming of the Son of Man be. For as in the days before the flood, they were eating and drinking, marrying and giving in marriage, until the day that Noah entered the Ark, and did not know until the flood came and took them all away, so also will the coming of the Son of Man be."

I'm praying for a hunger and a thirst for God. Judgment will one day come unexpectedly. We must live like Christ might return at any moment, because He will!

Today, God is calling people to come out of Babylon. People are going to repent, and they're going to humble themselves. They're going to desire a move of the Spirit more than anything in the world.

There's a theme now in America called "Make America Great," but it's shallow. Why? The only thing that's going to truly make America great is a Great Awakening of repentance, of holiness, of reverence for God, and a move of the Holy Spirit. God is going to send another Great Awakening. We must prepare our lives to be part of it.

QUESTIONS FOR DISCUSSION

✧ What are some ways Christians become complacent in their faith? In what ways have you found yourself becoming complacent in living for the Lord?

✧ One way to fight complacency is to remember your first love, the time when you first believed in Jesus. Think back and recall how God changed your life. What was different? What do you need to do to return to your first love?

✧ Why do plagues and times of struggle cause us to reconsider how we are living spiritually? How is God calling you to live differently in response to challenging times in your life?

✧ How can you help another person refocus on a true relationship with Christ? Ask God today to show you how to allow His Spirit in you to change the lives of those around you.

THE BABYLONIAN REBUKE
IN THE PLAGUE

The principles of God's Word are universal for every generation. They don't change at all.

Consider the word "Babylon." It comes from the word Babel, from the Tower of Babel in Genesis 11. It was man's first religious attempt after the flood to revolt against God and to establish his own perspective, his own religion, and his own power.

The Tower of Babel was man's attempt to build something for God to impress Him. The picture of Babel is one of humanity. God confounded their language, because He detested what they were trying to do. He wasn't impressed.

In Christianity, there are over 10,000 denominations. Every person who reads these words probably knows someone who has been part of a church split. Do you know why that happens? The nation of Babylon became a symbol of what we're going to discuss in this chapter.

When the Bible refers to the heart of Satan, you must remember that he was religious. Satan was a worship leader. He wasn't rejecting his religion or his worship; he rejected God's supreme authority in his life. His attitude was, "I'll set up my throne above Your throne. I'll be like the Most High." It's a picture of rebellion in the human spirit of flesh on the throne of our lives, even if it's religious flesh.

Let me share a Scripture with you from Daniel 4:13-17:

"I saw in the visions of my head while on my bed,
and there was a watcher, a holy one, coming down
from heaven. He cried aloud and said thus:

'Chop down the tree and cut off its branches, Strip off its
leaves and scatter its fruit.
Let the beasts get out from under it,
And the birds from its branches.
Nevertheless leave the stump and roots in the earth,
Bound with a band of iron and bronze,
In the tender grass of the field.
Let it be wet with the dew of heaven,

And let him graze with the beasts

On the grass of the earth.

Let his heart be changed from that of a man,

Let him be given the heart of a beast,

And let seven times pass over him.

'This decision is by the decree of the watchers,

And the sentence by the word of the holy ones,

In order that the living may know

That the Most High rules in the kingdom of men,

Gives it to whomever He will,

And sets over it the lowest of men.'"

Nebuchadnezzar begins by giving praise to God. He explains why he's glorifying God and giving praise to the kingdom of God. It's because Nebuchadnezzar experienced a rebuke from the Lord. In this rebuke, it started as a dream and as a revelation. God wanted to communicate to Babylon, to the world system, through the king of Babylon.

He wanted to communicate a warning to the religious world, and He did it by giving the king a dream. Nebuchadnezzar saw a beautiful tree. Then he saw this tree cut down and stripped, and its fruit taken away. He saw it bound and restrained.

The king called upon the prophet Daniel to explain the dream to him. What did it mean? When Daniel came, he shared God's revelation. Daniel 4:20-25 notes:

'The tree that you saw, which grew and became strong, whose height reached to the heavens and which could be seen by all the earth, whose leaves were lovely and its fruit abundant, in which was food for all, under which the beasts of the field dwelt, and in whose branches the birds of the heaven had their home—it is you, O king, who have grown and become strong; for your greatness has grown and reaches to the heavens, and your dominion to the end of the earth."

"And inasmuch as the king saw a watcher, a holy one, coming down from heaven and saying, 'Chop down the tree and destroy it, but leave its stump and roots in the earth, bound with a band of iron and bronze in the tender grass of the field; let it be wet with the dew of heaven, and let him graze with the beasts of the field, till seven times pass over him'; this is the interpretation, O king, and this is the decree of the Most High, which has come upon my lord the king: They shall drive you from men, your dwelling shall be with the beasts of the field, and they shall make you eat grass like oxen. They shall wet you with the dew of heaven, and seven times shall pass over you, till you know that the Most High rules in the kingdom of men, and gives it to whomever He chooses.

"And inasmuch as they gave the command to leave the stump and roots of the tree, your kingdom shall be assured to you, after you come to know that Heaven rules. Therefore, O king, let my advice be acceptable to you; break off your sins by being righteous, and your iniquities by showing mercy to the poor. Perhaps there may be a lengthening of your prosperity."

Nebuchadnezzar, a symbol of the world system, was first given a warning. After this warning, he was given a rebuke or a correction. This warning was given by the people of God and the Word of God.

Notice that the days of this world system were numbered and would come to an end, but God would allow it to continue for a while longer if Babylon would hear His rebuke. This was not yet the fall of Babylon; it was the rebuke of Babylon. It was a rebuke of the religious world system, just as Jesus rebuked five of the seven churches in Revelation as we mentioned earlier. It was a rebuke of the institutions, the governance, and the works of the religious world.

In a similar way, I am warning the smooth-talking pastors that your days are numbered and your time is coming to a close. You need to recognize what is true, what is eternal, and what matters. You

MIKE EVANS

need to reorder your values because Babylon, this world's system, is coming to an end. A day is coming when Babylon is going to be overthrown and Babylon is going to fall.

God spoke and gave the king an opportunity to repent, an opportunity to break off his sins by being righteous, and by showing mercy, so that there might be a lengthening of their prosperity before the Babylonian system fell completely. It was a warning to Babylon.

This is a great warning to every nation, tribe, kindred, and tongue going all the way back to Babel when all the nations had one language. Then God divided the nations by language to keep them from cooperating to rebel against Him. Likewise, all our systems have now been rebuked.

I wish I could tell you that Nebuchadnezzar's reaction to the warning was repentance and a change of heart, but it was not. Notice what happened in verses 28-32.

> "All this came upon King Nebuchadnezzar. At the end of the twelve months he was walking about the royal palace of Babylon. The king spoke, saying, "Is not this great Babylon, that I have built for a royal dwelling by my mighty power and for the honor of my majesty?"
>
> While the word was still in the king's mouth, a voice fell from heaven: "King Nebuchadnezzar, to you it is spoken: the kingdom has departed from you!

70

And they shall drive you from men, and your dwelling shall be with the beasts of the field. They shall make you eat grass like oxen; and seven times shall pass over you, until you know that the Most High rules in the kingdom of men, and gives it to whomever He chooses."

How long does God plow? He plows until the ground is ready. It lasts until we consider the plague of our own heart. Once God has decided to bring forth His plans, He does not waste time. Consider how quickly His judgment came upon Nebuchadnezzar in verses 33-36:

"That very hour the word was fulfilled concerning Nebuchadnezzar; he was driven from men and ate grass like oxen; his body was wet with the dew of heaven till his hair had grown like eagles' feathers and his nails like birds' claws.

And at the end of the time I, Nebuchadnezzar, lifted my eyes to heaven, and my understanding returned to me; and I blessed the Most High and praised and honored Him who lives forever:

For His dominion is an everlasting dominion,

And His kingdom is from generation to generation.

All the inhabitants of the earth are reputed as nothing;

71

He does according to His will in the army of heaven

And among the inhabitants of the earth.

No one can restrain His hand

Or say to Him, "What have You done?"

At the same time my reason returned to me, and for the glory of my kingdom, my honor and splendor returned to me. My counselors and nobles resorted to me, I was restored to my kingdom, and excellent majesty was added to me. Now I, Nebuchadnezzar, praise and extol and honor the King of heaven, all of whose works are truth, and His ways justice. And those who walk in pride He is able to put down."

This is a great review of the religious world system! It's a tremendous rebuke of Babylon. Nebuchadnezzar's pride was fully expressed in his claim that the whole world was his. It was all built by his hand. It was all built for his glory. It was built for his splendor. It was all about him and his pride and what he wanted.

Then there was a tremendous shaking of this king of Babylon who represented the world system. The Bible says his tree was chopped down, the branches were cut off, the leaves were stripped, and the fruit was scattered. It says that the creation that had gathered the birds of the air and the beasts of the field under the Babylonian system were scattered. It's a picture of the Lord rebuking the religious world's system. All the fruit of the flesh was restrained and stripped and the fruit was removed.

This is a time right now where there's a rebuke of the Babylonian system that's taking place. Here's what God has to say to the church: Get Babylon out of your heart. Get the Babylonian value system, the Babylonian priorities, and the Babylonian perspective out of your heart. This Babylonian system of the world that operates without God is going to fall.

This system has been revealed and exposed. We've looked so strong. We were growing. We were a mighty tree full of fruit. Everything looked wonderful. Now, suddenly we have been stripped bare. Our current plague has shown us how fragile this system really is.

Nebuchadnezzar thought everything was about him. Then he suddenly discovered that everything could be gone in a moment. The king who ate the delicacies of his time was quickly in his field on his knees eating grass. The king who had slept in beautiful palaces was now sleeping on the ground which was covered in dew.

The purpose was to shake Nebuchadnezzar's perspective regarding God's authority and glory. This is God's message to us as well. God wants the First Church of Babylon to be shaken. He wants our pride to be shaken. Just as with the king of Babylon, God will do whatever it takes to change our perspective toward Him.

The Lord started with a warning and a dream. Daniel then

offered a call to repentance, but Nebuchadnezzar didn't listen to any of that.

Then a shaking came. When his pride was brought low, all that he had boasted of was suddenly taken from him. It changed his view of himself and his view of God.

This is something that should already be a reality in the heart of the church. The church should already have such an exalted view of the Lord, but we often do not. As a minister, I really think we have seen the church as being small and the world as being big.

We have seen the world as having the good stuff, and the church as being secondary. We have seen the world as having the stuff that everybody celebrates and idolizes and for which people yearn. But now, this Babylonian system is being shaken. In the hearts of people all around the world, there's a great shaking taking place.

Those who have invested in this Babylonian system are being shaken to the core. Their view of Babylon and what it could produce and what it can do and its stability and its permanence has been shaken. Now hearts are being broken and people begin to lift their eyes to heaven.

The Word says that when Nebuchadnezzar lifted his eyes to heaven, his understanding returned to him. You won't believe what your eyes will see when this season is over. You're going to have opportunities you've never had in your life. The Holy Spirit is going to work in you with great power. Scripture tells us clearly in

Revelation that the kingdoms of this world are going to become the kingdoms of our Lord and of His Christ.

God wants the First Church of Babylon to be shaken and humble itself and repent of its prosperity and its pride and its arrogance and to repent. When we come to a place that we're so hungry for Jesus, so thirsty for a move of the Holy Spirit that we're willing to do anything, we're willing to repent, humble ourselves, and experience radical intercession, then we'll see and experience a Great Awakening.

The Lord has called us to holiness. There's a reason why we must lift our eyes up to heaven to understand that only God can be our strength. We can't take any of the glory.

We must be God's holy people filled with the fire of God, walking in the Spirit of repentance, who are small in our own eyes. I pray that the Spirit of God would touch you and transform you. I pray that the same Spirit that raised Christ from the dead will reveal truth to you and transform you for His honor and glory.

QUESTIONS FOR DISCUSSION

✧ In what ways do people act like Nebuchadnezzar today? How are we operating as if we are responsible for all our success rather than glorifying God?

✧ How did Nebuchadnezzar find restoration from his time of judgment? What can we learn from his response that we can apply to our own lives?

✧ What does it mean to be called to holiness? What are some ways holiness should look in your life today?

✧ How can you help someone you love to escape the temptations of Babylon? Ask the Lord to work through you to change the lives of others as He works in your own heart.

THE POWER OF THE CROSS

Have you noticed that a growing number of church buildings do not have a cross on the outside or the inside? Why are there no crosses?

If you look inside many modern churches, you rarely see a cross. Is there any significance to that? I can tell you, there is. It's called the power of the cross. Churchgoers don't realize it why there are few sermons on the cross, but I'll explain it to you. It's an incredible and powerful revelation.

When was the last time you heard a message on the cross, other than at Easter? The cross is central to our faith in Christ. The apostle Paul wrote in Galatians 6:14, "But God forbid, that I should boast except in the cross of our Lord Jesus Christ, by whom the world has been crucified to me, and I to the world."

I want you to think about this for a moment. The world had been crucified to Him, and it was because of the cross of Jesus Christ. In this Information Age, we find it difficult to understand. The idolatry of the Old Testament is incredible, that intelligent people could be so blinded that they'd offer worship to statues of stone and wood and metal. The Scriptures tell us that people walked up to a tree, cut it down to burn half of it and took the other part and engraved gods on it. The whole family would kneel before those images and pray to those gods to deliver them and to save them.

It was this sin of idolatry that brought down God's wrath on the children of Israel. It angered him more than any other sin in the Old Testament. God declared in Jeremiah 7:18, "The children gather wood, the fathers kindle the fire, and the women kneading dough, to make cakes for the queen of heaven; and they pour out drink offerings to other gods, that they may provoke Me to anger."

The situation angered God so deeply, that he commanded Jeremiah, "Therefore do not pray for this people, nor lift up a cry or prayer for them, nor make intercession to Me; for I will not hear you" (Jeremiah 7:16). This is God's declaration against idolatry in the Old Testament.

He hates idolatry just as much today. It brings His wrath and a generational curse. Now a new idolatry is sweeping across America. We don't see it, because it's very subtle and clever, and very religious, but it's idolatry. It's causing people to be distracted from an intimate relationship

with a personal God, and it's causing people to not repent and humble themselves in the presence of a holy Lord.

The New Testament warns us that ministers will come in the last days who will appear as angels of light, but who are instead ministers of Satan. These leaders will be charismatic, articulate, persuasive, and very resourceful, but they will not be of God. 2 Corinthians 11:13-15 predicts:

"For such are false apostles, deceitful workers, transforming themselves into apostles of Christ. And no wonder! For Satan himself transforms himself into an angel of light. Therefore it is no great thing if his ministers also transform themselves into ministers of righteousness, whose end will be according to their works."

Paul warned about these demonic spirits. He talked about preachers who would come and deceive people with a different spirit and a different gospel. He also spoke about the judgment of God that would come because of it. This deception is taking place today. That may sound shocking, but it's something you must prepare your hearts for, and receive by revelation from the Holy Spirit. When you hear reports of the Holy Spirit at work, you must evaluate the information.

If you lack discernment, you can be swept up into an idolatry that will turn you away from the cross of Christ.

Today you'll hear churches using sayings like, "It's about the team," or emphasizing that God wants you to prosper. It's partially true, but when God's Spirit falls upon the church, the emphasis is not on us; it's on the cross. I believe multitudes of Christians today are being deceived and swept into idolatry without even knowing it. They've been seduced by demonic angels of light.

Paul saw this beginning to happen. In Galatians 1:6-8, he warned:

"I marvel that you are turning away so soon from Him who called you in the grace of Christ, to a different gospel, which is not another; but there are some who trouble you and want to pervert the gospel of Christ. But even if we, or an angel from heaven, preach any other gospel to you than what we have preached to you, let him be accursed."

The words "let him be accursed" are strong. This is the great idolatry we are experiencing in our culture today. There are many preachers who have literally cast aside the message of the cross of Jesus Christ. It doesn't matter what anyone tells you about a great revival, or that God is really working, or the promise of a move of the Spirit that is taking place. It doesn't matter how many people show up in person or online. It doesn't matter how much money you have in your church, or how successful it appears. If the cross of Jesus Christ is not the door through which you come, you can rest assured that door does not lead to a holy God.

The cross, including its demands and hopes, is the very heart of the gospel. Any movement or church lacking the revelation of the cross is idolatry. Such worship is another spirit, another gospel. God will reject it. Without the cross, all that is left is chaff, a twisted message from the pit of hell. It's idolatry, more insulting to the Lord than that of ancient Israel. In most churches where this other gospel is preached, the rooms are filled with smiling faces. All the right words are sung and spoken. They use the right statements and have very pleasing messages, yet there is no conviction and no repentance. Let me be clear: If the revelation of the cross gets into your spirit, it will transform you. If you experience the reality of the cross, its confrontational aspects require change in your life.

Even when the cross is mentioned by these false teachers, there is no confrontation of sin. It's not the true preaching of the cross. If I were to preach about the demands of the cross in a church today, with its death to all worldly pleasures, many would flee just as they did when Jesus told them of the cost of following Him. If I were to teach to the comfortable megachurches of America, "God demands you to face your sins and kneel at the cross and deal with your wickedness," most would leave offended and never return.

As author A.W. Tozer wrote, "No one is a friend to the man with a cross." Such churches never even mention the cross. Instead, they pour their energies into worldly advice amplified by new technology. We're experiencing an entire generation of intelligent young ministers who are leading churches to build attractive facilities and grow their social media, but fail to emphasize what Jesus taught—that we are to take up our cross and follow Him.

God must cringe at the weak attempts of such churches to transform a lost and dying world. God help those ministers if they refuse to warn their people to forsake their sins! Jeremiah lamented that they also strengthen the hands of evildoers so that no one turns back from his wickedness. Jeremiah 23:18 says, "For who has stood in the counsel of the LORD, And has perceived and heard His word? Who has marked His word and heard it?"

Ezekiel taught that we are to be watchmen on the wall. We must watch and warn, or the blood of the people will be on our hands. God has looked down upon a sick world of people bound in a prison of fear and death, despair, full of doubt, without peace, groping in darkness and confusion, yet He sent His Son Jesus Christ.

Matthew 11:28 says, "Come to Me, all you who labor and are heavy laden, and I will give you rest." Jesus extends an invitation of the cross. It's a call to every sinful and weary soul bound in chains, pretending to live the abundant life when they're miserable and fearful and depressed.

As I prayed and repented before God during the coronavirus pandemic, God gave me a revelation of the cross. I saw Jesus hanging on it. In my spirit, I saw myself on the cross with him. Then I saw Him dying and me dying and being buried. I saw both of us being resurrected. I've never before seen it this way. It was a very shocking revelation. The Holy Spirit revealed that I must understand that I am in fact, crucified with Christ. I am buried with Christ and resurrected with Christ. If that revelation doesn't get deep into your spirit, you'll never live a victorious Christian life. You'll be defeated.

I know that you are weary from dragging your chains around. You're exhausted from sleepless nights. Yes, sin is a hard taskmaster. "Come to me now, with all your heavy burdens," He says, "and I will give you rest"—but go through the cross. Jesus died on the cross to forgive our sins, but also to take us through His crucifixion, His death, and His resurrection.

I met with evangelist Leonard Ravenhill just before he died. He asked me, "Are the things you're living for worth Christ dying for? Are you living your life in the light of eternity, so you don't fear eternity?"

Our sins weary the flesh. They make us weak and sick. Sin takes away all that is good and precious. Sin hardens the heart, destroys peace, and causes guilt, sorrow and shame. It consumes the mind with weakness, and makes the soul dark. It brings fear, and leads to scandal and heartache. Sin ultimately leads to death. Worst of all, sin shuts us out of communion with God.

Jesus said, "And I, if I am lifted up from the earth, will draw all peoples to Myself" (John 12:32). This lifting up of the earth Jesus mentioned was His crucifixion. He was lifted up before the whole world on the cross. It was an image of His great sacrifice for our sins.

When you talk with someone addicted to pornography, there is shame. What once captivated their attention and brought pleasure has now become an addiction that controls their life. What started as something they thought they could turn loose has become a chain around their neck and has destroyed their life and their spirit.

The body of Christ is not a huddle for the saints; it's a hospital for sinners. When sin-sick patients arrive and are told they're fine just as they are, that's blasphemy. God causes us to expose our wounds and our sins and be healed. Those solutions are not found in the song on the screen or by our clever sermons. They are found on our knees before a holy God.

If people are confronted with the Holy Ghost in power, they'll cry out and repent. I realize some ministers may be offended, but the offense of the cross is of greater importance than the offense of others. It's much more than simply leaving out stories about the cross. You can share the verses and still avoid the revelation.

Yes, I know ministers preach salvation and tell sinners outside the church to repent. I'm not talking about that. I'm talking about sinners in the seats inside the church. The cross is essentially a confrontation against man's sinful nature. Our sin should convict us, not comfort us. Look at what Jesus taught in John's Gospel:

John 14:6: "I am the way the truth and the life. No one comes to the Father except through Me."

John 10:9: "I am the door. If anyone enters by Me, he will be saved, and will go in and out and find pasture."

John 10:1: "Most assuredly, I say to you, he who does not enter the sheepfold by the door, but climbs up some other way, the same is a thief and a robber."

There's not much preaching today on holiness in the church. Why? Because pastors don't consider that believers can live a holy life. They just avoid it and then call it legalism.

Jesus Christ was crucified—and you were crucified with Him.

He was buried—and you were buried with Him.

He was resurrected—and you were resurrected with Him.

If you grasp that revelation, you will take up His cross. It will produce a sanctified life, and you will no longer be comfortable; you'll be convicted by the Holy Spirit.

A thief will promise you that you don't need to change. "Everything is just fine. God loves you just as you are. You don't need to change a thing." Today a pastor can be caught in adultery and still not even lose his job. A pastor can have an affair and be remarried two or three times. He just packs up and goes to another location. There's often no true repentance and change. He simply deceives one flock and then moves on to another. No wonder our churches are dying and broken! How can the sheep live healthy and safe if the shepherd is in deception? If you do not master your sins, your sins will master you.

Jesus didn't give us an easy message. He made His expectations clear. The Holy Spirit must reveal to you the revelation of the cross and your personal sanctification. If you aren't willing to be crucified with Christ, be buried with Christ, and be resurrected with Christ, you might have a born again experience of the cross, but will spend the rest of your life frustrated and miserable because you'll never come into the fullness of God. It's not about you becoming stronger; it's about you becoming weaker. We are to surrender it all to the cross. Luke's Gospel is clear:

Luke 9:23: "Then He said to them all, 'If anyone desires to come after Me, let him deny himself, and take up his cross daily, and follow Me.'"

Luke 14:27: "And whoever does not bear his cross and come after Me cannot be My disciple."

Yes, we are to love everyone. When it comes to being a servant of Christ, however, Jesus says that unless you deny yourself and follow the way of the cross, you are not His disciple.

Are you caught in a cycle of sin? Maybe it began with one little thing and now you can't stop. You lie and hide and cover up. Yet you feel comfortable in church because you're not convicted. God wants to send the Holy Spirit into your life and your church so that people will rise from their seats and cry out, confessing their sins.

I was with a group of Christian leaders meeting with Ronald Reagan and his entire cabinet for lunch right after he became President. One of my friends there that day was a minister who preached the message of the cross very strongly. He and I left afterwards for the Hilton Hotel. When the hotel doors opened, we walked inside. A lady working there was vacuuming and looked over at him.

She stopped the vacuum cleaner, fell on her knees, and cried out with tears. "God forgive me. I'm a fornicator!" She shouted it right in the middle of the lobby! The Holy Ghost came and touched her strongly. She didn't care what anybody thought or said. She was in the presence of the cross. It created a revelation that transformed her.

The world is waiting for you to die to self. It's waiting for you to surrender completely to the cross of Christ and to take up His cross.

Jesus says that we must deny ourselves, not indulge ourselves. To embrace the death of the cross and follow our Savior in repentance means more than, "Lord, I'm wrong." It means, Lord, You are right." Repentance is facing the consequences of our sins. We must be willing to do anything to change. Be willing to hang on a cross with Christ, to die with Christ, to be buried with Christ, and to be resurrected with Christ. When the Holy Spirit convicts you to this degree, your world will be changed. God loves you too much to allow you to remain in your sins.

Self-denial is not a popular message today. Self-fulfillment is. We've shifted from asking what is right to asking what feels right. If you want God's favor in your life, it will come at a cost. Psalm 1:1-2 teach:

> "Blessed is the man
> Who walks not in the counsel of the ungodly,
> Nor stands in the path of sinners,
> Nor sits in the seat of the scornful;
> But his delight is in the law of the LORD,
> And in His law he meditates day and night."

Two things are clear. First, we must reject living in sin. Second, we must embrace the Word and let it be alive in us. It's more than simply reading your Bible or memorizing a few verses. It's a life filled with and focused on Christ living in you, the hope of glory. When your prayers are stronger than your pleasures, a transformation takes place. The sin that held you back is now behind your back.

You cannot be taken to your knees by sin when you're on your knees in prayer. The glorious truth of the gospel is that if we die with Jesus, then we'll also come into the glory of His resurrection and newness of life. His cross is our cross. His death is our death. His resurrection is our resurrection. That's the revelation of the cross.

Yet this is the cross that many churches have abandoned. The cross is more than two overlapping sticks of wood; the cross breaks the chains of sin that bind us. I once heard a minister share a word about the pressures he had seen young ministers face in building large churches, the pressure each week to have more people than the week before.

He shared an ugly but honest truth: What it took to get people there is what it takes to keep people there. In many large churches today, here's what's happening on Sunday night after the services: The staff has a big conference call and compare notes. They share with each other tips on what's working and what's not. They do it for everything—the sermon, the worship, the sound, the lighting. The church has become comparable to the world. It's another Fortune 500 company.

It's a church built upon hype, smooth words, never confronting sin. You can draw people in with popularity, but it's a house of cards that's destined to fall. Think of it this way: What would a church look like in Sodom and Gomorrah? It would be a prosperous church. You say, "Well, I think I know what it would look like. It would have to compromise. It couldn't preach against sin."

One young evangelical leader quickly built a church of 10,000 people with captivating speaking, charisma, and leadership. Yet he was hiding secrets. He was a clever preacher, but he was completely defeated.

The public didn't know it. His preaching was smooth. The music was great. The church was growing. Everybody was applauding him. Then the preacher died in New York City in a hotel from a cocaine overdose. When you build your ministry upon sand, the storms are going to knock it down. We must build our lives on the rock, with Jesus Christ as our foundation.

When the apostles were arrested for preaching the gospel, a Jewish teacher named Gamaliel offered powerful words of wisdom that relate to us today. Acts 5:38-39 shares:

> "And now I say to you, keep away from these men and let them alone; for if this plan or this work is of men, it will come to nothing; but if it is of God, you cannot overthrow it—lest you even be found to fight against God."

When a movement is built upon God's power, it's unstoppable! The unsaved will find you. Pastor, if you can explain the growth of your congregation by human means, it's unlikely it is a move of God. If your plan is of men, it will come to nothing. But if God is at work in you and your people, there will be no other explanation than that the glory of God has manifested itself. It will shake your city and shake the world.

It all begins and ends with the cross. We need a revelation of the cross, or we'll never live a sanctified life. Proverbs 28:13 says, "He who covers his sins will not prosper. But whosoever confesses and forsakes them will have mercy." There is a lot of preaching today on the prosperity gospel, but you don't hear preaching on repentance as a key to prosperity.

Confession is like working out or running or lifting weights. It leaves us in agonizing pain when we begin. But when we keep going for two days, three days, one week, one month, after a while we become healthy and whole. Repentance is more than a one-time thing. It's something we must regularly do.

When we see the glory of God and the cross, our response is to walk in a spirit of repentance. We can't avoid it. Repentance hurts. The cross inflicted terrible pain because it was the death of the flesh. But when we humble ourselves and acknowledge we're wrong and He's right, something glorious happens.

Any person who sticks with Christianity only if things are going his or her way is a stranger to the cross. We must endure if we desire to follow Him. Is there a sin that's holding you back? Is it pressing you down like a heavy weight, robbing you of joy and peace? Then come to the cross! Paul wrote that he was crucified with Christ (Galatians 2:20). He had brought his sins to Jesus, the One who could destroy them through His work on the cross.

Maybe you've tried every method to remove your sin in your own power. You've tried accountability. You've prayed. You've tried every method and program and read books and videos and have sought counseling, but you're still defeated. You can't stop sinning. Take it to the cross, and leave it there. Your self-discipline will never lead you to victory apart from Christ. It will never deliver you from an unholy life. You need the supernatural revelation of the death of Christ, the burial of Christ, and the resurrection of Christ.

King David, a shepherd boy, discovered his defining moment when he faced a giant. Goliath stood taller than any soldier in the army, but David defeated him. He won the battle because he put his faith in God, not in himself. No one, including King Saul, wanted to face that giant. They feared defeat. What they forgot was that their power was not limited to what they could do, but what the Lord could do through them. David said, "The Lord is my shepherd, I shall not want" (Psalm 23:1). Against all odds, he used a sling and a rock to destroy his greatest enemy. The finest life is a person who has lived by the power of God.

There's another rock you also need to remember. On the first day of the week after Jesus was crucified, women came to the tomb. They wondered who might move the rock and roll the stone away. When they arrived, the rock had already been moved. The one who died on the cross was not defeated by the cross. The power of Jesus was so strong, that even death could not hold Him back. Let me challenge you today. Bring your sins to the cross.

Jesus will not let you down. He will forgive you. He will change you. He will transform you completely.

As Reverend Billy Graham noted, the ground at the foot of the cross is level. We must each come before the Lord to deal with our sins. I want to end this chapter with a prayer for you. I'm asking God to give you a revelation of the power of the cross.

Maybe you've never read a message like this. Until recently, I had never shared a message like this. Then God brought me on my face for weeks in repentance. I thought, "Lord, why are you doing this to me? I love you. I read your Word. I'm obeying you. Why are you doing this to me?" Do you know what happened? I got close to Jesus. I got close to the Holy of Holies. I got close to the throne room of God. The closer I got, the dirtier I felt. Why? Because my flesh is not holy.

If you are not being convicted, it is an indication of how far you are from the glory of God and the cross of Christ. You may be saved, but you're not sanctified. You're not living a holy life. You haven't died to self.

As I mentioned earlier, Leonard Ravenhill said two things to me during our last visit together. First, he pointed his finger at me and asked, "Are the things you're living for worth Christ dying for?" Then he asked, "Are you living your life in the light of eternity?" Then he brought me into his room. He lay back in his bed, because he was dying, and looked up. I followed his gaze and saw that he had written the word "Eternity" on the ceiling.

Are you living your life focused on eternity? If you are, you're going to be a part of a Great Awakening. The Great Awakening is coming with a revelation of the cross, with godly repentance, with radical intercession, and divine interruptions.

QUESTIONS FOR DISCUSSION

✧ What would the power of the cross look like in the life of a Christian today? What about in your own life?

✧ In the Bible, David defeated Goliath by relying on God's power despite overwhelming odds. What is an area that feels overwhelming in your life at the moment? How do you need God's help to overcome this challenge?

✧ How can we live focused on eternity? What are one or two specific ways this would look like in your life?

✧ God changes us to change others. Who is God calling you to serve? What is something you can do today to begin reaching this person or group of people?

THE MYSTERY OF THE CROSS

I n Galatians 2:20, Paul shared, "I have been crucified with Christ; it is no longer I who live, but Christ lives in me; and the life which I now live in the flesh I live by faith in the Son of God, who loved me and gave Himself for me."

This is more than a Scripture; it's a revelation. In prayer, I heard the Lord say, "My children will see the power of the cross in the Third Great Awakening."

You might be saying, "I've seen that already. I'm saved. It was at the cross that I understood it brought me to Christ."

That's something entirely different. Paul said, "I have been crucified with Christ." The person of the Holy Spirit can never be used to endorse or affirm anyone other than Christ: not your church or your pastor, not your ministry, or my ministry. Here's the problem: When we accept Christ, we do it genuinely. But for many of us, that is both the beginning and the end of our Christian walk.

After that, we're finished with the cross. It's ancient history in our life. We think it doesn't have any relevance today, but it does. Without the revelation of the cross, it is just religious flesh on the throne of your life, putting you at peace with your sins. We must humbly admit that all these attempts to live in our own strength are obstacles to the glory of God. We can accomplish more in one day when we get this revelation of being crucified with Christ than in a lifetime of sincere religious intentions.

You hear preaching on grace all the time. Why is there so much preaching on grace? Because the church is filled with defeated people bound in sin. Grace is needed, but so is sanctification. Sadly, many preachers are often just trying to find a way to make people happy.

I believe in the grace of God, but the refusal to surrender complete control of our lives to Christ and His cross is a declaration of war against His Lordship. When Christ resides in His rightful dwelling place in our heart, we are open to the Lord and to His will.

Today, the Christian life is often like a sandwich between sensuality and selfishness. Everyone's trying to convince everyone else that we're in revival and that God is moving. We're trying to assure everyone of it, but it's not really happening.

There is a place that you can reach spiritually, where you are in fact declaring what Paul said: "I am crucified with Christ." But for it to happen, the mountains constructed by religious fleshly pursuits must come down so that the valleys in our lives can be filled with God's glory.

One day fully surrendered to the cross of Christ can transform your life. It takes self off the throne, and chaos is no longer the norm. You're no longer living a religious life, pretending to be something you're not. You're not making provisions for your flesh, even your religious flesh. You're seeing Jesus.

One of the most important things to God is manifesting his Son fully and completely through our lives. For that to happen, we must see the revelation of the cross. Satan tries to keep us from it. He doesn't want us to understand it.

When we deny ourselves, take up our cross and follow Him, we are moving into a new realm of sanctification. Why don't preachers preach on sin anymore? Because they don't think believers can live victoriously. They're not perfect; no one's perfect. Galatians 5:2 begins with a powerful reminder that if we live according to anything except Christ, and Him crucified, it profits us nothing.

We want to hear pleasant things, messages on grace and forgiveness. Meanwhile, a plague of immorality has swept into the churches of America. The divorce rate is as high in the church as outside of it. Pastors don't preach against adultery because too many members are involved in it. They don't preach against pornography, because they have members bound by it who would stop giving to the church.

They don't preach about R-rated movies, because too many go to them, where the name of the Lord is spoken in vain, and the scenes dishonor the Lord.

As followers of Christ, we realize there's a lost and dying world that needs to see Jesus through us. Paul said, "Walk in the Spirit, and you shall not fulfill the lust of the flesh" (Galatians 5:16). The antidote to sin is the Spirit. We're not good enough or strong enough to stop sinning in our own strength. But God is Spirit. When we walk in the Spirit, we overcome the lust of the flesh.

What does it mean to walk in the Spirit? I'm a swimmer. I swim most days, perhaps 250 miles a year. I really enjoy it, but if someone came up and told me, "I'm a swimmer," yet refused to get into the water, or just stood in the water but didn't move around, I would not consider that person a swimmer. You can talk and sing about the Holy Spirit, but that is not the same thing as walking in the Spirit.

The apostle Paul also talked about the fruit of the Spirit. Galatians 5:22-23 record:

"But the fruit of the Spirit is love, joy, peace, longsuffering, kindness, goodness, faithfulness, gentleness, self-control. Against such there is no law. "

Walking in the Spirit seems obvious to those of us who love God, but there is more to observe in these words. The Greek word for "fruit" can also be translated "results." These traits are the results of walking in the Spirit. We don't perform them in our own power or strength. We don't exhibit love, joy, and peace simply because we're good people.

The world will tell you the power is within you to think positively. You're told not to worry, that you have grace, and God loves you just the way you are.

God does love us as we are, but He doesn't want us to stay as we are. The power is not within us. That's a lie from the pit of hell. The power is found in the cross of Christ. He suffered dearly on that cross for you. Our world teaches that you're smart enough, strong enough, and good enough. You don't need anyone's help. That's religious, secular humanism.

In some churches, the only requirement for a blessed life is giving money. You pay your tithes to the church, and you are promised a blessed life.

Christ offered a completely different message. Jesus told us apart from Him, we can do nothing (John 15:5). Yes, He also promised all things are possible with God (Matthew 19:26). Without Christ, we will fail. With Christ, we cannot fail, because our God is victorious.

Galatians 5:24 says, "And those who are Christ's have crucified the flesh with its passions and desires." When we walk in the Spirit, we show the results of it by exhibiting the fruit of the Spirit. It's no longer only Christ on the cross. Our human flesh is dead. We have been crucified with Christ.

Do you feel like sin is still holding you back? You may have accepted Him, but have turned your back on the cross. Nail your sins to the cross today.

There's another aspect we must understand regarding the mystery of the cross, and it's the way of the cross. This issue is addressed very directly in Romans 6:1-2: "What shall we say then? Shall we continue in sin that grace may abound? Certainly not! How shall we who died to sin live any longer in it?"

The false idea was that if God's grace abounds when we sin, sinning more would result in more grace. Is this true? Of course not! If we've truly repented, we will not have an attitude that says, "Let's sin more."

The next verse describes the solution to sin. Romans 6:3 shares, "Or do you not know that as many of us as were baptized into Christ Jesus were baptized into His death?" Believers who identify with baptism in this creation have declared the death of the old man. We have been crucified with Christ.

It's the work of the cross that produces sanctification. It's called the holy life. Sanctification is the process of being set apart from sin. We are raised from the dead with Jesus. We're overcoming temptation. We're living victoriously because we live by His power. It's the same power that created the sun and the moon and the stars (Genesis

1-2). God can work through you to transform your life and the lives of those around you. You don't have to pretend you are strong enough; He is able to strengthen you.

I've written before about living in the favor of God. If you walk in the Spirit, you'll have the favor of God, but that favor doesn't come easily. Look at 2 Timothy 3:12: "Yes, and all who desire to live godly in Christ Jesus will suffer persecution."

When was the last time you heard preaching or teaching on suffering? It's not very popular these days. But in the next Great Awakening, those willing to endure suffering and persecution will be those who will transform the world.

I had lunch one day with the late Oral Roberts. He told me, "You go into war zones, where the fire is the hottest, and the gift of faith is ignited, just as the apostles rejoiced that they were worthy to endure suffering for Christ." We can find indescribable joy through living in the Spirit, walking in the Spirit, dying to our flesh, living crucified with Christ, and following the way of the cross.

Many in today's generation don't really understand this. My dear friend David Wilkerson said, "Some Christians are content to merely exist until they die." They don't want to risk anything to believe or grow or mature. They refuse to believe that His Word is alive. They have become hardened in their unbelief. Now they're just living to die.

We're created to do more than merely exist. Yes, there's a cost to living godly in Christ Jesus. This cost is not designed to make us turn and flee. Instead, it should fill our hearts with joy and happiness when we stop pretending. I've seen this hunger in crusades. I remember one event where I cried out to God, "Give me a breakthrough in this nation or bury me, God." Little did I know that I'd be standing in front of five miles of people, 2.3 million people, proclaiming the word of the Lord, setting captives free.

Leonard Ravenhill, whom I mentioned earlier, a dear and mighty man of God spoke into my life just before he died. His words are so powerful. He told me, "No man is greater than his prayer life. The pastor who's not praying is playing. The people who are not praying are straying. Fail here, we fail everywhere."

It's a wonderful revelation that only the Spirit of God can give you. Out of this revelation comes repentance deep in your heart and soul. You're going to get a revelation of the glory of God. You're going to see the power of God. When the First and Second Great Awakenings took place, it was because of the revelation of the cross. The Third Great Awakening will be no exception. We must see the revelation of the cross.

Look at your fruit, or your results. Is the world being transformed because of you? Be honest with yourself. When you're willing to be crucified with Christ, and buried with Christ, then you will be resurrected with Christ. Our spiritual forefathers wept and prayed agonizing prayers before the Lord, asking Him to change the world.

As recorded in the book of Acts, many gave their lives for that change to take place. The answer to their prayers was that the message of the good news of Jesus quickly spread across the known world.

They were willing to pay any price to obey God. There weren't any exemptions for suffering. They wrestled in prayer until they had a breakthrough. Lost men and women were converted through their prayers of repentance. Will we again see the revelation of the mystery of the cross?

In Luke 24, the resurrected Jesus appeared to two disciples on the road to Emmaus. We are told one was named Cleopas, but the name of the other man is not given. They did not recognize Jesus when he began walking with them, but they were profoundly impacted by Him: "And beginning at Moses and all the Prophets, He expounded to them in all the Scriptures the things concerning Himself."

Notice that when Jesus wanted to change the lives of His followers, He turned to the Scriptures. He began with Moses and the Prophets, speaking about the Messiah. When they later recognized that it was Jesus, verse 32 shares, "Did not our heart burn within us while He talked with us on the road, and while He opened the Scriptures to us?"

When we fill ourselves with the words of Christ, our hearts will burn with the fire of God. The prophet Jeremiah said it best: "But His word was in my heart like a burning fire Shut up in my bones; I was weary of holding it back, And I could not" (Jeremiah 20:9).

When we fill ourselves with the living word, we will change our world. Charles Spurgeon, the great British preacher of the nineteenth century, talked about the desire to "bleed" God's Word when cut by the world. He wrote of British writer and preacher John Bunyan and said, "Prick him anywhere—his blood is Bibline, the very essence of the Bible flows from him. He cannot speak without quoting a text, for his very soul is full of the Word of God."

Wouldn't it be amazing to be known as a man or woman of God, whose very essence flows with the living words of God? Not just quoting Scripture with our mouth, but living it? That we died with Christ, and were resurrected with Him. Pastor Henry Blackaby says revival is when God's people return to God and God returns to them, and everyone sees the difference.

Yet, we must count the cost of genuine revival and awakening. We must be willing to make the commitment to crucify the works of the flesh, to know the way of the cross, and be consumed by our living Christ. We live in a world filled with Bibles, Bible teaching, and worship music. Why is the world not being transformed? It won't be until we are consumed by the fire of God and the cross of Christ.

Rightly understood, the words of Christ will always lead us to the cross of Christ. The cross is the foundation. You're not going to get away from it. Yet this is the problem with so many Christians and churches today. They've built on foundations other than the cross.

If your foundation isn't the cross of Christ, you can't hide it. You surely won't hide it from God. There will be a day when each one of us is going to stand before the Lord. He'll look at us and remind us that He was crucified, buried, and resurrected. What about you? Will you be able to say you died to self and lived the crucified life of Christ? Then the truth will be revealed.

I'm afraid too many believers will appear before the Lord filled with regrets. There's a world crying out for deliverance, and they're only going to be delivered through the power of His resurrection. If you're building your life on any other foundation than Jesus Christ, it's not going to last. Your hidden sins will be revealed; your fake exterior will be exposed. Why wait to address the sin in your heart? Come to the cross. Come to the revelation of the mystery of the cross.

You're not meant to carry your burdens alone. You're not meant to hide behind a wall of good religious intentions. They're just a mask. The life that you have comes from the Father, and it flows through the cross. Jesus said that we are to love the Lord with all our heart, our soul, and our mind. What is in your heart, your soul, or your mind that needs to change to love Him completely? We must be crucified with Christ, be buried with Christ, and be resurrected with Christ to the point we can shout, "Hallelujah, I died!"

Have you ever been in a worship service when God's Spirit moved and people started confessing lies, prejudices, addictions, and affairs? There is tremendous repentance.

Have you ever seen this happen with pastors? Maybe not, but I have. But I've only seen it when the Holy Spirit has taken complete control of a church. If man is in control, it will not happen.

Jesus will forgive you. He will cleanse you. He'll sanctify you, but it's through the cross. Psalm 86:5 says, "For You, Lord, are good, and ready to forgive, And abundant in mercy to all those who call upon You."

When we confess, Jesus takes our sins and nails them to the cross, and they're no longer part of our record. They are forgiven and forgotten. We must embrace this revelation of the cross. We hear of the goodness of God and of love in churches today, but we don't hear messages on hell. It's as if there is no hell. But there is! The last two Great Awakenings included fiery preaching on hell. As I mentioned earlier, Jonathan Edwards even entitled his most famous revival sermon "Sinners in the Hands of an Angry God."

Jesus came to deliver from sin. He is the only way. John 14:6 proclaims, "I am the way, the truth, and the life. No one comes to the Father except through Me." Romans 6:10-11 add, "For the death that He died, He died to sin once for all; but the life that He lives, He lives to God. Likewise you also, reckon yourselves to be dead indeed to sin, but alive to God in Christ Jesus our Lord."

We're talking about resurrection when you don't fear eternity, because you're living in it. Paul wrote in Romans 8:10, "And if Christ is in you, the body is dead because of sin, but the Spirit is life because of righteousness." It's the Spirit of Him who raised Jesus from the dead who dwells in you. The Spirit that resurrected Christ also brings life to us.

You rarely hear a message on sanctification. Why not? Because you can't live a sanctified life without the cross. If you are not crucified with Christ, buried with Christ, and resurrected with Christ, you'll attempt to live the Christian life and struggle your entire life with the flesh. God has more for you than that. Come back to the cross. May God give you this revelation that will change you, your family, your church, your city, and the world!

QUESTIONS FOR DISCUSSION

✧ This chapter asks, "What is in your heart, your soul, or your mind that needs to change to love Him completely?" How do you respond to this question?

✧ Why do you think so few people live a life fully committed to the Lord? What are some of the barriers that get in the way?

✧ Growth happens better in community. What are some ways you can grow with other Christian friends?

✧ When the cross changes us, we become motivated to share Christ with others. Who do you need to share Christ with today? Read 1 Peter 3:15-16 and be prepared to share the reason for the hope within you.

THE PROMISE OF THE SPIRIT, PART 1:

A HEAVENLY POWER SURGE

But this is what was spoken by the prophet Joel:

'And it shall come to pass in the last days, says God,

That I will pour out of My Spirit on all flesh;

Your sons and your daughters shall prophesy,

Your young men shall see visions,

Your old men shall dream dreams.

And on My menservants and on My maidservants

I will pour out My Spirit in those days;

And they shall prophesy.

I will show wonders in heaven above

And signs in the earth beneath:

Blood and fire and vapor of smoke.

The sun shall be turned into darkness,

And the moon into blood,

Before the coming of the great and awesome day of the LORD.

And it shall come to pass

That whoever calls on the name of the LORD

Shall be saved.'" (Acts 2:16-21)

God promised He would send the *ruach hakodesh*, the Hebrew words for the Holy Spirit. He sends it so we don't face the burdens in our own power, because trying to do the Lord's work in our own strength is the most confusing, exhausting, tedious work possible. But when we're filled to overflowing with the Spirit of the Lord, it's completely different. Strength flows out of us. I want you to understand the promise, the power, and the purpose of the Holy Spirit in the life of the believer, especially in the time of a plague. Why? Because God gave us the promise of the Holy Spirit.

When was the last time your sons and daughters prophesied? When was the last time old men dreamed dreams? That would be me. I'm dreaming dreams. This is what happens when God fills the house, our temple, and the church. Throughout the Scriptures, God promised that He would send a spirit into the hearts of people to accomplish His purposes.

In the Old Testament, God told the prophet Ezekiel, "I will give you a new heart and put a new spirit within you; I will take the heart of stone out of your flesh and give you a heart of flesh. I will put My Spirit within you and cause you to walk in My statutes, and you will keep My judgments and do them" (Ezekiel 36:26-27).

Think on that for a moment. Do you have a stone heart? You might, but you will see your heart differently in the presence of Jesus. Every knee will bow and every man will humble himself and see what they're not. In the New Testament, Jesus declared in John 7:37-39:

> "If anyone thirsts, let him come to Me and drink. He who believes in Me, as the Scripture has said, out of his heart will flow rivers of living water." But this He spoke concerning the Spirit, whom those believing in Him would receive; for the Holy Spirit was not yet given, because Jesus was not yet glorified.

After His resurrection, Jesus told His followers in Acts 1:7-8:

> "It is not for you to know times or seasons which the Father has put in His own authority. But you shall receive power when the Holy Spirit has come upon you;

and you shall be witnesses to Me in Jerusalem, and in all
Judea and Samaria, and to the end of the earth."

The word "witnesses" is from the Greek word *marturos* from
which we get our word "martyr." Jesus told them they would be
living martyrs for Him in Jerusalem, Judea and Samaria, and to the
uttermost parts of the earth. Why did He say "living martyrs"? It
was because those who are crucified with Christ are martyrs, but
those resurrected with Christ are living martyrs, filled with the
Holy Spirit.

Jesus didn't want His church to face life without the Holy Spirit.
The same promise of the Holy Spirit is given to you, as well. Let me
give you an example of the power of the Holy Spirit. A lot of people
think they have the Holy Spirit. You might have Him, but the Spirit
doesn't have you. You've defined what it means to be filled with the
Spirit, but you have no comprehension of what happens in a Great
Awakening.

One time, the Holy Spirit told me to go to Somalia. There was no
desire in my heart to travel there, but I responded in obedience to
God. While there preaching the gospel, a Black Hawk helicopter was
shot down. Terrorists were firing everywhere, with warlords ruling,
and machine guns mounted on their pickup trucks.

Some terrorists spotted me and started chasing me. I was running, but there was nowhere to go. There were around two dozen

terrorists pursuing me, and I'm six foot six, trying to outrun them and hide. I had no way to defend myself, and ended up sprinting toward an old abandoned airport runway.

I prayed, "God, deliver me, deliver me!" Suddenly, I saw a twin-engine plane landing. I reached into my pocket where I had kept a $100 bill. As soon as the plane stopped, I waved the money in front of the pilot and said, "Take me with you."

He asked, "Where are you going?"

I answered, "Anywhere!" He opened the door, I jumped in, and the plane took off. If that plane had not arrived at that exact moment, I would have most likely died that day. The Holy Spirit delivered me. God can send the power of the Holy Spirit into your life to rescue you and to transform you.

The Bible sometimes mentions darkness like a plague. Remember what God says in Isaiah 60:1-2:

"Arise, shine;

For your light has come!

And the glory of the Lord is risen upon you.

For behold, the darkness shall cover the earth,

And deep darkness the people;

But the Lord will arise over you,

And His glory will be seen upon you."

The Lord knew that we would need the power of the Holy Spirit to stand victorious and pure in a dark world. The Holy Spirit is available today to empower us. For example, the Holy Spirit led me in 1980 to travel to Israel to visit a discouraged young man whose brother had been killed. I was led to pray over him that he would become the Prime Minister of Israel, and he did. His name is Benjamin Netanyahu. The Holy Spirit told me to do that. I didn't know Benjamin. I didn't know what my assignment was, but I obeyed God. I just obeyed God.

You have no comprehension of the assignments God has for you if you will come to the point where you deny yourself and live crucified and resurrected with Christ. What will come out of your spirit? What will come out of your heart and mind? It will be like a supernatural antenna, with direct contact with God!

I want to say something to those of you who are pastors. Do you want the Holy Spirit to fill your church? Are you sure? Do you want that kind of an anointing in your church? Because it's going to mess up your program. You're not going to have everything scripted. When the Holy Spirit shows up, people will repent. They will be on their faces before the Lord. The Holy Spirit will interrupt your music, and even your message. Are you sure you want it? The world will be changed if it happens, but you must be willing to risk it all.

The Holy Spirit served as the great Comforter and strength to the early church. After one of the first major persecutions, the church went into prayer. The Bible records that when they prayed, the place where they were assembled together was shaken. They were all filled with the Holy Ghost and spoke the word of God with boldness (Acts 4:31).

Paul the apostle also relied on the power of the Holy Spirit in his ministry. In 1 Corinthians 2:1-5, he wrote:

"And I, brethren, when I came to you, did not come with excellence of speech or of wisdom declaring to you the testimony of God. For I determined not to know anything among you except Jesus Christ and Him crucified. I was with you in weakness, in fear, and in much trembling. And my speech and my preaching were not with persuasive words of human wisdom, but in demonstration of the Spirit and of power, that your faith should not be in the wisdom of men but in the power of God."

There was a reason Paul relied on the power of the Holy Spirit. He said your faith should not be in the wisdom of man, but in the power of God. Are we relying on the power of the Holy Spirit today? Or do we rely on our traditions? Our wonderful, lovely traditions offer very inspiring worship and messages, but they are no substitute for the power of God.

Paul noted in verse 4, "And my speech and my preaching were

not with persuasive words of human wisdom, but in demonstration of the Spirit and of power." In 1 Thessalonians 1:5, he added, "For our gospel did not come to you in word only, but also in power, and in the Holy Spirit and in much assurance, as you know what kind of men we were among you for your sake."

In 2 Timothy 3:5, Paul warned one of the signs of the last days would be a powerless gospel: ". . .having a form of godliness but denying its power. And from such people turn away!"

Sometimes, people doubt healings. But when you see healings, things change. I was praying one day and the Spirit of God said, "I'm going to open up Africa to you. You're going to lead crusades all over Africa."

So I thought I was headed to Africa. But then God said, "First, you're going to the Mexico, to the Acapulco Princess Hotel, and you're going to pray."

I told my wife, "God's going to open up Africa, but first I'm supposed to go to the Acapulco Princess Hotel in Mexico and pray." Carolyn knows I really try hard to obey the Lord, so she approved, despite how odd the request sounded.

While I was there, I was walking outside and a couple strolled toward me. When they got close, I turned to the lady and said, "You know an African president with a tremendous need in America and you don't know how to solve the problem. But I've been sent to do it for you. I'll take care of that matter."

The woman turned to her husband and asked, "Dennis, did you talk to him?"

He replied, "No, I didn't. I don't even know this man. Sir, what's your name?"

I told them and his wife said, "What you said is absolutely startling! My name is Maureen Reagan. My father is the President of the United States, Ronald Reagan. I'm the chairwoman of the Republican Party. I've been sent to Africa to meet with all the African presidents. The last one I met with wants to come to America and share his plan for democracy with the press, but no one will receive him."

I repeated, "I'll take care of that." I returned to my room and called the leader of the National Religious Broadcasters, Ben Armstrong. I said, "Ben, I want you to include a certain African leader on the platform the day that Ronald Reagan speaks at the Hilton Hotel."

He agreed. I ended up hosting the President and his cabinet in my room before he spoke at the NRB convention. I'll never forget it. The African leader later said to me, "I don't believe in Jesus because I've seen a lot of fake preachers come into the country and exploit it."

So I got on my knees and I repented. He said, "No, no, it wasn't you. What must I do to get you off your knees?"

"Accept Jesus," I said. "That will work." I led him to Christ right there in the room! That opened the nation of Africa. We later held a crusade in Uganda. We went to the Congo with another crusade. We traveled all over Africa, but it happened because the Holy Spirit said to go to the Acapulco Princess Hotel and pray.

God has a mighty purpose for the Holy Spirit in your life. Joel 2:32 reveals, "And it shall come to pass That whoever calls on the name of the LORD Shall be saved. For in Mount Zion and in Jerusalem there shall be deliverance, As the LORD has said, Among the remnant whom the LORD calls."

There's a reason for the promise of the power of the Holy Spirit. It's so that the people of God can bring the truth of God to a world desperately in need of the hope of God, through Jesus Christ. The Holy Spirit is given to enable us to experience powerful transformation in our lives, the life of our church, of our nation, and of our world, to be a living martyr, as a witness to the Lord. The power of the Holy Spirit is sent to give you a revelation of a living word, not just any word.

Jesus counselled His disciples, "I still have many things to say to you, but you cannot bear them now. However, when He, the Spirit of truth, has come, He will guide you into all truth; for He will not speak on His own authority, but whatever He hears He will speak; and He will tell you things to come" (John 16:12-13).

The Holy Spirit comes to strengthen us through His presence. John 14:16-17 says, "And I will pray the Father, and He will give you another Helper, that He may abide with you forever—the Spirit of truth, whom the world cannot receive, because it neither sees Him nor knows Him; but you know Him, for He dwells with you and will be in you."

Do you want to walk in the promise, the power, and the purpose of the Holy Spirit?

Then, you will have to humble yourself and repent. You must recognize you're an empty vessel, not a filled one. In 1972 I was in Texarkana, Arkansas, and I saw an older lady carrying her suitcase into the hotel. I ran up to her and asked, "Can I carry this for you, ma'am?"

I found out later that the woman was Corrie Ten Boom. She looked at me and said, "Young man, you can carry it if you will have some soup with me."

We entered the hotel and sat down for some soup. She said, "Tell me your story." I told her my testimony. She cried. She told me hers and I cried.

I remember asking her during that time, "You've had so many answers to prayers. Has there ever been a prayer you prayed that God did not answer?"

She said, "Only one." She shared that she wanted her family's Ten Boom clock shop to be a witness for the Lord. At the time, it had been sold to a secular company.

After she died, the Lord spoke to me in the Spirit. He led me to go to Haarlem, Holland, and purchase the Ten Boom clock shop to answer Corrie's last prayer. When I traveled to Holland and talked with the owner, the man was not a believer. It was around 11:45 or so in the morning. I said, "Sir, would you sell me the clock shop so I can make it into the 'hiding place' for Corrie and her beloved family who saved 800 Jews and invested 100 years praying for the peace of Jerusalem?"

He answered, "No, It's my clock shop."

I asked, "May I pray?"

"Yes, if you would like."

I started praying. As I did, all the clocks went off in the clock shop. He stopped me and asked, "Do you know what's going on?"

I said, "Yes, the clocks are going off."

"Yes, but you know what day it is?" He asked.

"No."

"It's April 15, the day that Corrie Ten Boom was born and the day she died."

The Lord had sent me there on the very *day* she was born and had died. He said, "I will sell it to you." And he did. We had everything restored. It has been open ever since as a witness for the Lord. It is all for the glory of God.

But I want to tell you something that really touched me. On the day we met, Corrie told me, "I was 51 and in solitary confinement when I prayed, 'Jesus, tomorrow's my birthday. There's always a big party for me.'"

The Lord spoke to her that day and said, "I have a gift for you for your birthday. It is the last verse of Psalm 91."

I didn't look it up until that day, April 15 in Haarlem, Holland. Psalm 91:16, the last verse of Psalm 91, reads, "With long life I will satisfy him, And show him My salvation." Corrie was 51 years old when God gave her that promise. She died at 91 on her birthday, April 15. The gift was 40 more years of life in ministry to change the world. That's what the Holy Spirit can do in our lives. That's the power and the purpose of the Holy Spirit.

QUESTIONS FOR DISCUSSION

✧ Many powerful stories are shared in this chapter. When was a time God worked through a powerful story in your life that you knew was led by His Spirit?

✧ When Paul wrote that He knew nothing but Christ and Him crucified, how does that encourage you today? How does the simplicity of Christ and the power of His Spirit change the way we live?

✧ Why do you think so many people do not live a life filled with the Spirit of God?

✧ What will you do to follow God's Spirit to live for the Lord today?

THE PROMISE OF THE SPIRIT, PART 2:

WHEN HEAVEN INVADES EARTH

When the Holy Spirit comes, you are changed forever. When the Holy Spirit invades every part of your life, you cannot remain the same. But for this to happen, the human spirit must be dethroned. This can only happen through the Holy Spirit.

Even a religious human spirit on the throne of your life is a declaration of war against the Lordship of Jesus Christ. A hunger for the power of the Holy Spirit will require you to acknowledge your need of more of the Holy Spirit. Acts 2:1-2 records: "When the Day of Pentecost had fully come, they were all with one accord in one place. And suddenly there came a sound from heaven. . ."

You can't accomplish the work of God, no matter how sincere your beliefs, without the power of the Holy Spirit. Jesus' disciples were timid. They were also very religious, but they were cowardly, afraid, hiding in the upper room, and had even betrayed the Lord. Their weaknesses had been exposed, and they were painfully aware of their condition.

This lasted until a sound came from heaven. Heaven can do what earth cannot. Only the battles you win in the spirit realm can be won in the physical realm. In 1983, the Lord told me to go to Lebanon. At that time, terrorists were everywhere in that country. There weren't just one or two terrorist organizations—there were dozens. It was perhaps the most dangerous spot on the planet to visit in 1983.

I took a fellow with me who I thought was going to be my prayer partner. I came back

To our room around 10 at night and he was sound asleep. I asked him, "Are you ready?"

He answered, "Oh, no, we're not going anywhere. The Israeli intelligence called up and told us there's going to be a terrorist attack tomorrow at the place we are going."

I said, "I know God told me to go."

He said, "I can't go because my insurance will be canceled."

I asked, "Did you say your assurance or your insurance?"

The next day, I rented a bus with an Israeli license plate on it. I drove through Israel all the way to Beirut, Lebanon, following the road signs because I don't read Arabic. I ended up preaching to U.S. Marines in Beirut. I'll never forget it. They were all just kids, 18 to 20 years old. I shared the Gospel and gave them Bibles. There was one young man from Massachusetts that I led to the Lord. I had a camera crew with me, so he asked, "Can I say something to my mom?"

He shared, "Mom, I'm not coming home for Christmas. But I know you've been praying that I'd find Christ. I want you to know I have just accepted the Lord Jesus Christ as my personal Savior."

That night, I slept in a sleeping bag on the sand in an area by the sea. All the Marines had returned to their barracks. Early in the morning I heard a massive explosion that killed all those Marines.

A huge battle followed. I was in Beirut, but I had a vehicle with an Israeli license plate on it. The troops told me I had to get out of there. I tried to drive back to Israel and ended up in the middle of a Hezbollah funeral. These were Hezbollah terrorists that had been killing Jews. I had two men in the car with me. They kept saying, "We're dead."

I said, "No, you're not dead. You're still talking." I was driving as fast as I could, because terrorists were spotlighting our vehicle and shooting 135-millimeter shells, trying to blow it up. I didn't really know where I was going because I couldn't spot the sea. Instead of going toward Israel, I was driving towards Damascus. We ran out of gas and our car was lit up with a spotlight from a terrorist on a nearby hill.

I jumped out of the car to remove the Israeli license plate. I unscrewed the license plate, and climbed back inside the car. The shells were flying all around us. Suddenly, a young man young man about 18 or 19 years old came right up to our car window. I thought he was an Arab terrorist and was going to kill us. He looked at us and then lifted his hand. I thought it was going to hold a gun, but it was a can of gasoline, which he poured it into our tank.

He came back around and pointed his finger towards the button, wanting us to open the car door. He never talked. I opened the door and he entered our vehicle. He led us toward the border of Israel, down dirt roads as the enemy fired at us. When we started pulled up to the border, the military guard there said, "We thought you were dead. We knew you went in, but we never thought you'd come out. How did you survive?" I turned to acknowledge our Arab rescuer, but he was no longer in the car.

Yes, that has been the only time in my life I believe I may have experienced a real angel. The humor of it is that he was dressed up like a young Arab terrorist, but he wasn't. I think he was an angel of God sent to deliver us.

When the Holy Spirit comes, the breath of God is released in your life. There's a sound from heaven like a rushing mighty wind. It will fill your house and your being. God will breathe on you, giving you life and breath.

We all need a rushing mighty wind to blow through our lives, to blow through our churches, to blow through our homes and our businesses, to bring the breath of God into the empty flesh of our lives with His power and His purpose. The prophet Ezekiel saw a vision when he wrote:

Also He said to me, "Prophesy to the breath, prophesy, son of man, and say to the breath, 'Thus says the Lord God: "Come from the four winds, O breath, and breathe on these slain, that they may live." So I prophesied as He commanded me, and breath came into them, and they lived, and stood upon their feet, an exceedingly great army (Ezekiel 37:9-10).

When the Holy Spirit comes, fire fills the church. Acts 2 says there appeared to them divided tongues as a fire. It came upon each of them and they were all filled with the Holy Spirit.

When the Holy Ghost comes in, pure hearts become ablaze with passion. When the Holy Spirit comes, empty hearts become overflowing. When the Holy Spirit comes, the church comes alive with the presence of God, and the timid and fearful become powerhouses of witnesses for Christ and His glory!

During the coronavirus pandemic, there was a series on ESPN called *The Last Dance* about Michael Jordan. There was one story, however, that wasn't told. It was my story. After Michael Jordan's father died, Michael was in a deep depression. He walked onto the floor of the basketball court crying on Father's Day. The young man was devastated over his father's recent death.

I had never met Michael Jordan, but I was in Orlando, Florida, having breakfast one morning when a basketball player came up to me and said, "Oh brother, I have to hug your neck." He was a big guy who must have been nearly seven feet tall.

I asked, "Do I know you?"

He answered, "No, cut do you remember when you held the pre-game chapel service with the Milwaukee Bucks and the Boston Celtics? Well, I found Christ. I was on the verge of divorce and bankruptcy. My life was radically transformed that night when you shared your testimony, and I never got to thank you. I just want to thank you."

I was honored and responded, "Thanks for sharing. That's very encouraging."

He invited me to join him for breakfast. As I did, I was shocked to discover that he was having breakfast with Michael Jordan. Michael had invited players there from the Orlando Magic, the Chicago Bulls, and the Boston Celtics for what he called Fantasy Camp. My new friend brought me up to Michael and said, "Michael, this preacher saved my life. I'm asking if he can join us for breakfast."

Michael said yes, and I sat down with them. As we were in the middle of eating our meal, the Holy Spirit came on me and whispered, "Pay the bill."

I walked up to the cash register and asked, "How much is their breakfast?"

The worker answered, "$1,135, not including the tip."

I cringed at the response, but continued to obey God's prompting to pay for the meal as well as a tip. As I left, my doubts increased. I felt like such a fool. "How could you be so stupid?" I thought. "You left halfway through the meal. You paid for all their food and they're mega-wealthy and you're not. What were you thinking?"

That afternoon around three o'clock, Michael Jordan's brother found me and said, "My brother was so moved at what you did. He wants to have dinner with you tonight with his wife and children."

That night, I sat with Michael, and shared Christ as I and talked with him about his dad and the Heavenly Father. What a glorious witness that was! Only the Holy Spirit could do that.

On one other occasion I was in Jacksonville, Florida, having breakfast. There was a man there eating breakfast alone and the Holy Spirit prompted me to join him. I didn't recognize the person, but I walked up, pulled out a chair, sat down, and said, "Good to see you again. What are you having for breakfast? Bacon and eggs? Me, too. How have you been?"

He answered slowly, "I've been great. How are you doing?"

"I'm great."

We began to eat together, and he said, "I'm a little bit embarrassed. I don't know who you are."

I said, "I'm a Holy Ghost hitman and God has a contract out on you." The guy's name was Jimmy Snyder, known widely as Jimmy the Greek. He had just lost his job as a sports commentator and a Las Vegas odds maker. I ended up leading him to belief in Christ that day. Only the Holy Spirit can set those things up. When the Holy Spirit comes, there's glorious transformation!

When the Holy Spirit came in Acts chapter 2, the church stopped hiding and spilled out into the world. The men of the world no longer intimidated the men of God. The world heard the message of the church and was convicted by the Spirit.

God wants the church to turn the world upside down again, because the world is wrong side up. This is only the work of the Holy Spirit. Acts 17:6 says, "These who have turned the world upside down have come here too."

I want to share one more very unusual story with you. Years ago, I left Orlando and was flying to Cleveland, Ohio, to preach. After boarding a flight on American Airlines, I sat in my seat, and promptly fell asleep. When I awoke, the pilot was saying, "We're now flying over Phoenix, Arizona."

I turned to a flight attendant and said, "That can't be right. There's no Phoenix, Arizona on the way to Cleveland, Ohio."

She said, "You're not going to Cleveland. You're going to Los Angeles." I was on the wrong plane!

I don't know how it happened, but it did. I landed in Los Angeles and then boarded an all-night flight to arrive in Cleveland on time to preach. I sat in my seat and all I wanted to do was sleep. But there was something I didn't know. The person in front of me was Pete Rose, the baseball player. The passenger behind me was John Glenn, the astronaut. The person next to me was a diplomat from the White House. There was a big event they were all traveling to attend. They were all on the same flight!

The diplomat beside me started talking with me as the flight began. At one point, I looked at him and said, "You have a hole in your soul."

He answered, "What?" I repeated my statement and he looked at the bottom of his shoe!

I said, "It's not the bottom of your shoe sole." At that moment, the Holy Spirit guided me. I told him, "My friend, you're married, but the woman you slept with last night was not your wife. You're an immoral man, committing adultery. You're a lost soul who needs Christ."

He turned pale and must have thought I was with the CIA or FBI. But on that flight, I led him to faith in Christ. As we talked about the Lord, Pete Rose would occasionally turn around to eavesdrop on our conversation. So did John Glenn.

When the plane landed, I realized I had not been on the wrong flight after all. I was exactly where God had placed me to serve as His messenger. I was led by the Spirit of God and I didn't even know it!

Is the Holy Spirit moving in your life like this? God wants to do it. Let Him do it. Let Him transform you. Let Him acknowledge you're empty, so the Holy Spirit can fill you. Let heaven invade your life and the life of your church.

The breath of God is ready to breathe. The fire of God is ready to fill you with purpose and passion and power. The church of God is ready to arise to the mission God has for it.

QUESTIONS FOR DISCUSSION

✧ Has there ever been a time when you've seen God's Spirit work in a way that can only be explained as supernatural? What happened? How did God glorify Himself through the event?

✧ What would it look like for your life to be completely controlled by God's Spirit? What is something specific that would be different?

✧ Name some of the temptations that attempt to keep you from living by the control of God's Spirit in your life. How can you overcome these temptations by God's power?

✧ Who is a person God is leading you to help? Ask the Lord for wisdom and obey as God opens an opportunity.

9

THE IDOLS ARE COMING DOWN

e're in the midst of a plague. One reason God sent the plague is so that the idols in our lives would come down. I want to share some Scriptures with you that are startling:

And do not become idolaters as were some of them. As it is written, "The people sat down to eat and drink, and rose up to play" (1 Corinthians 10:7).

"Little children, keep yourselves from idols. Amen" (1 John 5:21).

"But then, indeed, when you did not know God, you served those which by nature are not gods" (Galatians 4:8).

"The rest of mankind who were not killed by these plagues still did not repent of the work of their hands; they did not stop worshiping demons, and idols of gold, silver, bronze, stone and wood—idols that cannot see or hear or walk" (Revelation 9:20).

Do you see a theme in these verses? God's Word often speaks about idols. For example, in the Book of Revelation, one third of the population is already destroyed by chapter 9. However, two-thirds of the planet who refuse to repent during the plagues will be left behind.

Maybe you're thinking, "Well, that's in the future. I won't be here for that." But I want you to consider the question: Do you have any idols in your life?

Have you ever watched *American Idol*? Have you ever seen Hollywood stars at the Emmy Awards being idolized? Have you ever seen musical artists or sports figures like LeBron James idolized? Yes, there are many people who worship idols. There's a revelation in this that's much deeper. This all began with God dealing with me about idolatry. I didn't even know I had any idols in my life.

One time, I was on my way to India with one of my daughters.

After arriving at our hotel, we entered our rooms in preparation for a major outreach event. After falling asleep that night, I dreamed I saw the Lord sitting on His throne. He looked at me and then looked down. When He looked down, I saw idols—big ones, skinny ones, bad ones, and thin ones—all kinds of idols. The Lord said to me, "Whose idols are these?"

I thought these were the idols that the Indian people worshiped. But when I looked down at the idols, I saw my name on every one of them. I woke up crying at 1:30 in the morning, spending the rest of the night in prayer, feeling so unclean and unworthy.

When I attended the meeting the next night, there were thousands of Indian people, but I said, "I'm not even worthy to preach. I've seen the idols in my life and I've repented before the Lord." But that night a great miracle happened. Three girls who were born blind began to see. No one had prayed for them. I was just preaching "See Jesus" to the people, and suddenly they could see. The next night we had over a million people at that crusade. Why was there such a great breakthrough and tremendous awakening? God had worked by calling me to repent of idolatry.

I want to ask you a question: When was the last time you've repented of idolatry?

I'm firmly convinced in my heart that the number one reason the COVID-19 plague was sent is because of the idols in this nation and the world.

What is an idol? An idol is anything that captures our affection and our attention, and draws us away from intimacy with the Lord. Jesus talked about men or money being an idol, but the Jews weren't worshipping an idol of money. There were no idols of money at that time. Jesus saw the greed and the obsession for their prosperity as idolatry. He saw what the Puritan preacher Thomas Watson later declared. Watson said that in the first commandment, worshipping a false god is forbidden. However, the second commandment of worshiping the true God in a false manner is also forbidden.

Perhaps you've never heard a message on idolatry at your church. Why not? People don't think they have idols today, yet sometimes even our churches can become an idol. There are idols in all our lives that must be revealed by the Holy Spirit. There's nothing that enrages God and brings the judgment of God down more than idols in the lives of His covenant people.

However, most Christians don't even understand what idolatry is. God says in the second of the Ten Commandments, not to make an idol of any form above the earth or on the earth or beneath the waters. That's an amazing revelation. What does it mean?

Nothing should take the place of God. No material possession, not a nice car, a house, or a business. We are not to make idols, nor are we to bow down to them. It's one thing to make an idol; it's another thing to worship it, offering an idol enormous value that takes all your attention.

You might say, "I've never worshipped idols." But anything that captures your heart, adoration, or devotion and robs you of pursuing the presence of God is idolatry.

Every person has a hierarchy of values and has placed something at its apex. Whatever it is, that is the god you serve. How do you distinguish between the good and the bad? How do you measure the best from the worst? You have a standard of evaluation; those things that are important to you, including your religion.

We need to be reminded by the Holy Spirit to sift us and shake us and search us so that we're not robbed of the power and presence of intimacy with Christ. You don't hear preaching on sin anymore, or judgment, or holiness, or often not even the Second Coming of Jesus. Why not? Many have subscribed to a value system that's devoid of messages on holiness. It's not relevant anymore.

God's demand is that He has the rightful place on the throne of our lives. Jesus said we cannot serve two masters. When Paul wrote to the Gentiles, he mentioned the tremendous idolatry in the church. He told the believers in Ephesus that greed and coveting were idolatry. When created things take the place of the Creator that is idolatry.

What I share next may offend you, but there are many Christians who have allowed their church to become a form of idolatry. They've allowed their lovely edifice, their spectacular worship, their marvelous sermons, and everything else that takes place in the building to become an idol. They call the church the house of God, but it's not. The church facility is a building. The church is the body of Christ.

We must be very careful that we do not allow the world to deceive us into a belief system where we worship a type of golden calf. When you look at your church and your worship, and you're comfortable in your contentment, the only thing that's required of you is your tithe. If you pay it, you get to play. You get to move ahead, you get a ticket to heaven, and an exemption from hell. Even though you may be in sin, there's no preaching against sin. If you're giving money, you can be comfortable.

I'm not preaching against tithing, but I'm preaching against anything that robs you of the intimacy of Christ. When a good thing becomes overly important to us, it becomes a possession, and often an obsession. We get excited about it. We seek more of it. We surrender to that idol, and place human opinion above God and God's revelation. Man is flesh. All men are flesh.

I want to remind you of what David Wilkerson told me over breakfast in 1986 at the Embassy Suites at the Dallas-Fort Worth airport. He showed me a letter he wrote to PTL, the Christian television network which many looked up to at that time. Wilkerson said, within 12 months from the date of his letter, the judgment of God was going to fall and bats would fly through the empty buildings. It was 12 months from the day of that letter that the judgment of God fell on PTL. David Wilkerson said in the letter, "You are fornicating with brick and stone." It was idolatry.

Instead of accepting himself as a man made in God's image, the idolater tries to remake God into his image. He takes Christ and tries to bring Him down to a comfortable size. Jesus becomes a celestial Santa Claus in a fantasy world of comfort with judgment. There is no more fear of God, and no more fear of hell.

Remember the book of Revelation? It's written about events yet to come. I spoke earlier about Revelation 9:20. It shares that the rest of mankind who are not killed by these plagues still did not repent of the works of their hands. They did not stop worshipping demons and idols of gold, silver, bronze, stone, and wood.

How many people do you know who worship an idol of gold, silver, bronze, or wood? Nobody, right? We might not have friends doing this now, but Scripture predicts that people will.

When Solomon created the temple, he talked about its magnificence. He worshiped the Lord and declared the God of heaven cannot be contained in this earth. He can't live in a place made by human hands.

Many Christians cut God down to their size, destroying reverence and holiness. For example, in some churches there's a sense many times that the building is the house of God. That can become idolatry. It places man in control, and religious man on the throne comes at a terrible price.

Isaiah cried out that the people's idols had become a burden (Isaiah 46:2). Your idols are a burden to you because you carry them. Isaiah reminded those of his time that when God brought their forefathers out of Egypt, He carried them. Self-made men become terribly upset when others don't come to admire them and put the spotlight on them. They want the attention.

One problem in many of today's churches is that we have bowed down to the idol of popularity to please the world around us. We have become a seeker-friendly church. This is similar to what happened with the children of Israel. They lost their distinctiveness. God challenged them to "come out from among them and be separate," but these words were ignored. Churches face the tension of upholding the eternal revelation, yet communicating it to a lost and dying world. Each of us faces this tension not to get so caught up in our culture that we lose sight of the Lord.

I'll give you a perfect example of idolatry. I know President Donald Trump. I've been in the Oval Office many times. I've had dinner with the President, and I'm so grateful for all he's done for Israel. That's my passion.

But there are Christians who have made Donald Trump an idol in their lives. There are even preachers who have made him an idol in their lives. Not the Word of God, not the Holy Spirit, but a man of flesh. They have become so drunk on power that they push everything else aside. That's idolatry.

All our idols, all our attempts to whittle down God to fit Him into our way of doing things, to fit Him into a comfortable pattern that does not harm our own ideas, or challenge our way of thinking, cause us to lose the touch of God. There is no longer a Holy Ghost Great Awakening.

We know the story in Exodus 24 of how, upon leaving Egypt, the children of Israel fashioned a golden calf and worshiped it. But one of the things no one talks about, and that you've likely never heard, is that Aaron the high priest made that golden calf and used the word Yahweh to describe it. He was basically saying to them, "Let's all gather together and worship God. I have an image for you to use as a point of contact." They weren't worshiping a bull as some had done in Egypt. They were still worshipping God, but were doing so in the way they saw fit, rather than the way God required.

In outrage, Protestant Reformer John Calvin said the heart of man is a perpetual factory of idols, giving us the chance we'll replace God with any and every object, person, idea, or dream. We aren't beyond idolatry; sometimes we simply dress it up in religious clothes. It's anything that promises life or security or joy apart from God.

Idolatry engages the deepest emotions of our heart, and can be anything—sports, or television, or your gym. It can include your status, your business, your home or cars, your church, your pastor. Any image that comes between you and a holy God is idolatry. The irony here is that idolizing something ultimately keeps us from being able to enjoy it. You panic and fret about losing something so vital that you can't sleep.

Some of the wealthiest people I've ever known are tormented by their wealth. Pastor Charles Spurgeon said the Word of God is like a caged lion. If someone threatens the lion, you don't have to stop and defend the lion. Just let it loose and it will protect itself. The Word of God can protect itself, but our false idols always need to be protected.

If your business is your idol, or your status is your idol, you'll sacrifice your integrity to climb the ladder of success, even in your church or ministry. If acceptance is your idol, you'll sacrifice your integrity to get it. But, you will always lose.

You'll violate everything, including your marriage covenant, because of your idols. Your idols will never be satisfied. It's like fire; it's never enough. You cannot satisfy it. The altar of idolatry is terribly insatiable. The more you sacrifice to it, the more it will demand.

From where do you feel that pull to keep cutting corners or making excuses? Don't fool yourself and think that you are beyond temptation.

For pastors, I want to pray for you. Many of you have been in your churches and you pour out your heart, yet you're hurting. You're trying to survive. We need to surrender everything to the Lord. It's not about us. It's not about our stuff or our dreams. It's about Him. He doesn't need our stuff. We can't put the focus on our stuff, not even our messages. Believe it or not, God can operate just fine, even without our sermons.

A Great Awakening is coming. Even in a plague, God has a plan. Let's remove the idols that stand between us and our complete devotion to God so that He will work through us as part of His divine plan in these unprecedented days.

QUESTIONS FOR DISCUSSION

✧ What are some common "idols" you see people bowing to today? Which ones are most tempting for you?

✧ In what ways do idols fail to satisfy? How is this different from the satisfaction the Lord gives us when we place Him first in our lives?

✧ How are you tempted to put other idols or gods before the Lord? What is something you need to change to keep God as your number one priority?

✧ Who is someone God has placed in your life that needs to be encouraged to leave their idols and place God first? Pray and seek ways to help that person this week.

THE PLAGUE OF
THE HEART

W hen I have been on my face in repentance during the coronavirus pandemic, the Lord spoke to me that leaders all over the planet are saying COVID-19 is an invisible enemy which no one knew about, and that we must fight this invisible enemy. This is not only coming from one leader; those in charge worldwide are making similar remarks. Nobody could ever have seen something like this coming. That's what they're all saying.

But COVID-19 is not the invisible enemy. The invisible enemy is a spiritual virus that has kept everyone in the dark. With all due respect, somebody did know about it. God Almighty knew. The Word of God says, "And ye shall know the truth and the truth will set you free" (John 8:32). However, we don't usually look at the full story. Verses 31-32 read, "Then said Jesus to those Jews which believed on him, If ye continue in my word, then are ye my disciples indeed; And ye shall know the truth, and the truth shall make you free."

Do you see the difference? It's called the plague of the heart. The world was in a drunken orgy on New Year's Eve 2019. While they were celebrating, a few individuals in Wuhan, China came down with pneumonia. On January 11, 2020, the Chinese media recorded the first death, a 61-year-old man in Wuhan China, as later reported by the World Health Organization.

At least 400,000 people have flown to the U.S. from China since January 11, 2020. They have flown to San Francisco, New York, Los Angeles, Seattle, Newark, Chicago, and Detroit before the U.S. imposed travel restrictions. In a video clip from 2006, 14 years ago, the following words were shared:

"What do you think the likelihood is that there'll be a pandemic? If it happens, how bad do you think it will be? 15 percent said they thought there'd be a pandemic within three years. But much worse than that, 90 percent said they thought there'd be a pandemic within your children or your grandchildren's lifetime. And they thought that if there was a pandemic, a billion people would get sick. As many as 165 million people would die. There would be a global recession and depression as our just-in-time inventory system and the tight rubber band of globalization broke. And the cost to our economy of 1 to 3 trillion dollars would be far worse for everyone than merely 100 million people dying, because so many more people would lose their job and their health care benefits that the consequences are almost unthinkable."

Think about those words. How was this kept from the world? Why didn't we have this information? There is a reason we didn't know. Look at the following words from a 2005 video by President George W. Bush:

"Scientists and doctors cannot tell us where or when the next pandemic will strike or how severe it will be. But most agree, at some point we are likely to face another pandemic. And one day, many lives could be needlessly lost because we failed to act today. By preparing now, we can give our citizens some peace of mind, knowing that our nation is ready to act at the first sign of danger, and that we have the plans in place to prevent and, if necessary, withstand an influenza pandemic. A pandemic, an infection carried by one person can be transmitted to many other people. And so every American must take personal responsibility for stopping the spread of the virus."[1]

Isn't that shocking? In 2015, four world famous leaders, including Bill Gates, predicted that this was coming. In a video interview, Bill Gates said:

"Today, the greatest risk of global catastrophe doesn't look like this. Instead, it looks like this. If anything kills over 10 million people in the next few decades, it's most likely to be a highly infectious virus rather than a war. Not missiles, but microbes. Now, part of the reason for this is that we've invested a huge amount in nuclear deterrence, but we've actually invested very little in a system to stop an epidemic."

In the previous chapter, I shared about a Great Awakening in the Old Testament from 2 Chronicles 7:14. In this chapter, I want to share the same dedication from 1 Kings 8. I will also reveal what God told me will be the first signs of a Great Awakening in this nation during prayer.

---

1   From https://www.govinfo.gov/content/pkg/PPP-2005-book2/html/PPP-2005-book2-doc-pg1630.htm.

LESSONS FROM SOLOMON

When King Solomon dedicated the original temple, the house of God, He didn't appoint a priest or a prophet to pray. He did it himself, in the presence of the entire congregation. He knelt and humbled himself. He spread forth his hands to offer up prayer from a sensitive heart, to present it to heaven with both arms. He gave God the glory. He humbly acknowledged the incapacity of the house that had just been built.

After building a glorious temple, he shares, "But will God really dwell on earth? The heavens, even the highest heaven, cannot contain you. How much less this temple I have built!" (1 Kings 8:27). Solomon dedicates the temple and then he acknowledges something. We're coming to the most astonishing part that will change your life.

In 1 Kings 8:37-40, we read:

"When famine or plague comes to the land, or blight or mildew, locusts or grasshoppers, or when an enemy besieges them in any of their cities, whatever disaster or disease may come, and when a prayer or plea is made by anyone among your people Israel—being aware of the afflictions of their own hearts, and spreading out their hands toward this temple—then hear from heaven, your dwelling place. Forgive and act; deal with everyone according to all they do, since you know their hearts (for you alone know every human heart), so that they will fear you all the time they live in the land you gave our ancestors."

Notice, Solomon says, ". . .whatever plague or sickness there is." Then he adds, ". . .when a prayer or plea is made by anyone among your people Israel." This refers to either an individual or multiple people. Furthermore, he said that, "when each one knows the plague of his own heart" (KJV). Did you get that? He tells them, your prayers aren't going to work until each one of you knows the plague of his own heart and spreads out his hands towards the temple. Then in heaven, God's dwelling place, He will forgive and act, giving to everyone according to all His ways, whose heart you know. For God alone knows the hearts of all people.

Verse 40 continues, ". . .so that they will fear you all the time they live in the land you gave our ancestors." The word "plague" is used twice. He talks about the plague in the land and the plague in the heart. It's the same word. If the people of Israel who are praying or groaning under a national calamity, a personal calamity, a famine, a drought, or a plague, he tells them that their prayers would not be heard; it is judgment for sin.

Verse 35-36 adds, "When the heavens are shut up and there is no rain because your people have sinned against you, and when they pray toward this place and give praise to your name and turn from their sin because you have afflicted them then hear from heaven and forgive the sin of your servants, your people Israel. Teach them the right way to live, and send rain on the land you gave your people for an inheritance." He conditions the removal of the judgment as genuine repentance. He would not ask that their prayers might be answered unless they also turned from their wicked ways and repented, that each person would know the plague of their own heart.

SIN IS THE PLAGUE OF THE HEART

Sin is the plague of the heart. Indwelling corruption corrupts the spirit of man like a spiritual disease, and blinds him. He does not see what's coming, in the same way we did not see or the world did not see what was coming with COVID-19. We must repent and say, "God, search my heart. Root out of me my wicked ways and my idols."

How do you rid the plague of your heart? How do you stop it? The Center for Disease Control (CDC) is giving us a message: Stay home. Spiritually, the answer is the same: Stay home. Come back to your first love and cleanse your house with repentance. There are still many hard-hearted preachers that don't have a broken heart, and are filled with pride and arrogance, who have not been with Jesus, and who depend upon their gifts and the praise of man. They don't want to offend anyone. They don't want to declare, "Thus saith the Lord." They prefer entertainment. The poison in the pulpit is infecting the masses. Maybe you're thinking, "That's not my pastor. He preaches the

Word." Oh, really? How much does he preach the Word? Fifty-percent percent? Ninety percent? How about 95 percent? If he preaches the Word 95 percent of the time, five percent is a plague in his own heart, and that spiritual virus will infect everyone who listens to him just as does the coronavirus. Of course, there are many faithful pastors who continue to preach the Word. I am eternally grateful for these fearless leaders. Yet far too many shepherds watch the sheep for their own benefit rather than truly proclaiming God's message to transform the lives of those they are called to serve.

Jesus is coming back for a glorious church without spot or wrinkle, a blameless church, as He declares in Ephesians 5:27. It will not be a corrupt church, a compromising church, a comfortable church, a careless church, a closed-mouth church, a condescending church, a cowardly church, or a clever church.

I know a pastor who never mentions the name of Jesus in his messages. I don't know how he gets away with it. He says God, but he won't say Jesus. It's all about smooth, clever messages that are exempt from judgment. He promises blessings and protection from God's judgment if you pay to play. The attitude is that if you tithe, there will be no judgment.

This is not God's plan! God's will is to deliver us from sin, not by making us stronger and stronger, but by making us weaker and weaker. That's not what the pastors are preaching, but it's what God

Almighty is declaring. God sets us free from the dominion of sin, not by strengthening our old man, but by crucifying him; not by helping him to do anything, but by removing him from the scene of action. It's all about the cross.

THE LIE OF OUR CULTURE—AND THE CHURCH

Telling believers, "You're okay. God is for you. Everything will be fine," is a lie! It's a plague of the heart. At the age of 18, while I was in military service, I was living in Philadelphia. I was so thrilled. I had just come back from Korea. I had a car full of brand new clothes, custom-made, and I had saved my money. I had several thousand dollars in my lovely car, along with all my possessions. During a stop, I gave a tip to a parking attendant to watch my car for just five minutes.

I bought a cup of coffee to go. When I came back, my car was gone. Everything I owned was gone. I ended up sleeping that night on a cot at the Salvation Army with the homeless people I had passed on the street. The next week, I moved to the YMCA. I fasted for seven days with no food, only drinking water. I read the entire New Testament in seven days. At the end of those seven days, I read my first Christian book, *The Cross and the Switchblade*, by David Wilkerson.

I also remember that Christmas. I walked in the snow to attend church several miles away. There was a big snowstorm. I had $13.25 to my name. That was it. I put $10 in the offering and walked in that snow back to my room. Everyone was celebrating Christmas dinner. I stopped at a diner and only had $3.25. I noticed a sign for bacon and eggs for $3.25. That would be my lunch.

During that time, I had no control over my circumstances, but I had one thing: I had a heart burning for the Lord. With my Bible in that diner, the Spirit of God said to me, "Your eyes have not seen, your ears have not heard. It has not entered your spirit what I've prepared for you. I will reveal it to you by my Holy Spirit."

The Great Awakening is going to come, but it's not going to come before idols are smashed, or statues in a park are pulled down. One of the greatest idols in the church is the idea of control. This is the word of the Lord to you, pastor: God, not the devil, can shut down your church. I hear the voice of John the Baptist in John 3:10: "The axe is already at the root of the tree, and every tree that does not produce good fruit will be cut down.

What did God tell me about a Great Awakening? What will be the first sign? Believers will come out of their prayer closets of repentance, rushing into their churches. They won't arrive 10 or 15 minutes early, they will arrive hours early. They won't even be invited to come, but they'll be in the front of the church, flat on their faces, crying out to God. When you start seeing that in the churches, you will know it's the beginning of a Great Awakening.

STOP TOUCHING

The CDC also gives another warning to avoid the plague: Stop touching. The apostle Paul says:

> Therefore, "Come out from them and be separate, says the Lord. Touch no unclean thing, and I will receive you." And, "I will be a Father to you, and you will be my sons and daughters, says the Lord Almighty."

When was the last time you heard a message on holiness in your church? 1 John 2:15-16 teaches, "Do not love the world or anything in the world. If anyone loves the world, love for the Father is not in them. For everything in the world—the lust of the flesh, the lust of the eyes, and the pride of life—comes not from the Father but from the world."

Too many churches love the world and are copying it. There are consultants and experts to tell you how to "do church." One of the top pastoral executive search companies in America is run by a pastor who was kicked out of his church for immorality. Think about it. When was the last time you heard a message on hell, holiness, or separation from the world? When was the last time your pastor preached a sermon against sin, rebuking backsliders? When did you last hear a message on the cross?

2 Timothy 4:2 commands us to preach the Word, to rebuke, and to reprove. Preacher, if you promised an exemption from judgment to

your congregation if they would come to church and pay their tithes, that is Ichabod. That's what the Lord is saying: Ichabod. It means "no glory." My father attended church every Sunday, and faithfully tithed. I remember one winter he was out of work, and went to the bank to borrow the money he would have made for his tithe and gave it to the church. He never missed a Sunday.

Yet my father was living in sin. Every Friday night he was drunk, sleeping around with women. I have discovered only in recent years a half-brother and a half-sister because of this man. He thought he had an exemption because he tithed and attended church. The mafia goes to church. They never miss Catholic mass and they tithe, too. Stop making the size of your church a measurement of the blessing of God. It's idolatry. King Herod boasted of his great temple. However, he was cursed with gangrene, convulsions, and manic depression.

I know seven pastors of megachurches, including two in Chicago, who were all kicked out of their churches for immorality. What does that say about them? What does this say about a seeker-friendly church in the time of a storm about those who preach a non-confrontational gospel? Today, a person can be a Democrat, a Republican, a pornographer, or choose nearly any sinful lifestyle, and still be made to feel comfortable in church.

One recent study revealed 68 percent of Christian men in America view pornography. Worse, approximately 50 percent of pastors do as well!² Two-thirds of millennials have now left the church. Why? Because churches are not really growing people to spiritual maturity in Christ. They're swapping. One church swaps members with another church. People become unhappy and a couple thousand move from one congregation to the next. Then the pastors stand in the pulpit and tell their stories of success. It looks more like an Amway sales convention. But they are leaving out the most important thing; they're leaving out the truth.

One time, a pastor screamed at me in rage, "You've ruined my church!" Why? I stood up in his pulpit and commanded the spirit of homosexuality to come out of that church in the mighty name of Jesus. Thirty-six men who were homosexuals came running to the altar, crying and repenting. Four of them were married and one was an elder in that church. The pastor was horrified. We must be moved to the point where we repent of the sins of the heart and truly make Jesus our Lord and Savior.

I once met a Muslim in the Middle East that I will never forget. He came up to me and said he was a born again Muslim. I asked him where he went to church.

He responded, "Oh, I don't go to church. I go to the mosque."

"What do you mean you go to the mosque? I thought you were born again?"

He said, "I am."

---

2 From https://conquerseries.com/why-68-percent-of-christian-men-watch-porn/.

I challenged him, "Do you believe Jesus was crucified and resurrected?"

The man answered, "He was crucified, but He wasn't resurrected."

"How do you know you're born again?" I asked.

His response shocked me. "Because the pastor told me so."

Do you realize where you will stand before a holy God, pastor? You're telling a man he's born again. He's never been convicted of his sins. He hasn't truly repented, but you counted him as one of your converts.

BROKEN, REPENTANT PASTORS

Another sign of a Great Awakening will be broken, repentant pastors in the pulpit. Listening to pastors who compromise truth so that they can succeed in Sodom and Gomorrah is shameful. The church has not gone to war against the invisible enemy.

Because I do so much of my ministry in Israel, I receive hundreds of letters from Christians asking, "Is the temple being rebuilt? Because the Antichrist will come into it and he'll sit on the temple and masses will worship him."

The apostle Paul said in 2 Thessalonians 2:1-12 (KJV) teaches:

> "Now we beseech you, brethren, by the coming of our Lord Jesus Christ, and by our gathering together unto him, That ye be not soon shaken in mind, or be troubled,

neither by spirit, nor by word, nor by letter as from us, as that the day of Christ is at hand. Let no man deceive you by any means: for that day shall not come, except there come a falling away first, and that man of sin be revealed, the son of perdition; Who opposeth and exalteth himself above all that is called God, or that is worshipped; so that he as God sitteth in the temple of God, shewing himself that he is God.

Remember ye not, that, when I was yet with you, I told you these things? And now ye know what withholdeth that he might be revealed in his time. For the mystery of iniquity doth already work: only he who now letteth will let, until he be taken out of the way. And then shall that Wicked be revealed, whom the Lord shall consume with the spirit of his mouth, and shall destroy with the brightness of his coming: Even him, whose coming is after the working of Satan with all power and signs and lying wonders, And with all deceivableness of unrighteousness in them that perish; because they received not the love of the truth, that they might be saved. And for this cause God shall send them strong delusion, that they should believe a lie: That they all might be damned who believed not the truth, but had pleasure in unrighteousness."

The apostle Paul adds in 1 Corinthians 3:16, "Don't you know that you yourselves are God's temple and that God's Spirit dwells in your midst?" And 2 Corinthians 6:16 teaches, "What agreement is there between the temple of God and idols? For we are the temple of the living God. As God has said: 'I will live with them and walk among them, and I will be their God, and they will be my people.'"

Listen to what the apostle John includes in 1 John 2:18: "Dear children, this is the last hour; and as you have heard that the antichrist is coming, even now many antichrists have come. This is how we know it is the last hour."

Do you see the theme of these verses? There's always going to be a Christ on the throne of your life. It will be the Lord Jesus Christ or the spirit of the Antichrist, that plague of the heart. An antichrist spirit is a spirit of iniquity. It has already taken over the education system, media, the arts, the culture, the Internet, and the government. Now it's taking over the church. Remember when we used to have Wednesday night services and Sunday night services and revivals? Where are those?

In Matthew 24, the disciples bragged about the greatness of the Jewish temple. Yet Jesus answered them, "Many will come in my name. . ." That "many" represents an antichrist spirit, a plague of the heart. The word "antichrist" in Greek means reputation, authority and fame. For many, not *the* Antichrist, but an antichrist spirit shall come in my reputation, authority, fame, saying I am. The Greek word "ego" can be translated "I." These deceivers will say, "I'm anointed. God told me. God is with me." Yet they are deceiving people.

One prosperity preacher told me, "I need a plane to protect the anointing. If you walk in faith, you'll have a guarantee from heaven. And you'll be blessed. You can make a demand upon God." I couldn't believe his words!

Today, seeker-friendly churches have self-appointed prophets. What do they prophesy? They are filled with words of encouragement. Yet Jesus rebukes religious leaders 77 times in the New Testament. Thousands of preachers will be angry with me over this book, but so be it. I will not be a pimp to a prosperity pastor.

The apostle Peter declared judgment must begin in the house of God (1 Peter 4:17). In 2 Timothy 3:12 adds, "Everyone who wants to live a godly life in Christ Jesus will be persecuted."

The prophet Isaiah declared there were covenant people at that time who were slapping their hands in the face of a holy God because they were in love with the world. They were in Egypt. There were three prophets over a seven-year period in Israel. They were Jeremiah, Isaiah, and Ezekiel. Isaiah 30:1-2 teaches:

> "Woe to the obstinate children,"
>> declares the LORD,
> "to those who carry out plans that are not mine,
>> forming an alliance, but not by my Spirit,

heaping sin upon sin;

who go down to Egypt

without consulting me;

who look for help to Pharaoh's protection,

to Egypt's shade for refuge."

Verse 7 adds, "Therefore I call her Rahab." Do you know what "Rahab" means in Hebrew? It means "do nothing." God's talking to you, pastor. He's telling you that you've been a great voice, but you're not transforming the world; you're not seeing My face. You're copying other preachers. In verses 12-14, Isaiah adds:

Therefore this is what the Holy One of Israel says:
"Because you have rejected this message,

relied on oppression

and depended on deceit,

this sin will become for you

like a high wall, cracked and bulging,

that collapses suddenly, in an instant.

It will break in pieces like pottery,

shattered so mercilessly

that among its pieces not a fragment will be found

for taking coals from a hearth

or scooping water out of a cistern."

This is what the sovereign Lord, the Holy One of Israel says: Only in returning to me and resting in me will you be saved. I know this has been a strong and a hard word for pastors, but it must happen in the church. Remember the two signs: The first sign would be repentant believers rushing to their churches before services, falling flat on their faces, crying out to God. The second sign would be repentant pastors.

God has dealt with my own heart in the same way. He gave me this word of judgment and I've been lying on my face, repenting and seeking His face. I want you to hear what the Holy Spirit is saying. Remember the words of the old hymn:

"Softly and tenderly, Jesus is calling.

Calling for you and for me.

See all the portholes, He's waiting and watching,

watching for you and for me.

Come home. Come home. You are weary, come home.

Earnestly tenderly, Jesus is calling, calling,

oh sinner, come home."

QUESTIONS FOR DISCUSSION

✧ What does it mean to have a plague of the heart? How does God use plagues to turn us toward Him?

✧ Brokenness is not enjoyable, but it is sometimes necessary in our spiritual lives. In what ways have you felt broken before the Lord recently? How could God use this brokenness to help you better live for Him?

✧ Purity is an essential part of our spiritual life. Are there areas of purity you need to address in your own walk with God? If so, what do you need to change or confess?

✧ God changes us to change others. Who is God calling you to serve? Seek the Lord for direction for the person or group where you can be used to help better grow in Christ.

THE THIRD
GREAT AWAKENING

How does a Great Awakening look? Jonathan Edwards, the fiery preacher who led the First Great Awakening in America, wrote, "You hang by a slender thread with the flames of defined wrath flushing about." In Enfield, Connecticut, on July 8, 1741, 38-year-old American evangelist Jonathan Edwards delivered what became one of the greatest sermons ever preached in our nation. The title? "Sinners in the Hands of an Angry God."

According to George Thomas of CBN News, history records the people in Edwards' church came under such conviction that they gripped the pews. Some historians credit that single sermon by Edwards for sparking one of the greatest moves of God this nation has ever seen. It became known as America's First Great Awakening.[3]

It started with a series of revivals in the 1730s, largely fueled by the preaching of men like Jonathan Edwards and George Whitfield, an evangelist from England. The First Great Awakening accomplished in America what the Reformation did in Europe. It directed people back to a vital, living faith in God.

Up until that time, the colonists had taken their relationship with God for granted. The original Christian fervor of the first settlers had long since died away. That sense of call, that sense of urgency to come to America and put the gospel into practice and create a society with liberty and justice for every soul, had begun to ebb and slip away. Those troubled preachers like Edwards and Whitfield, who believed that God had a spiritual calling on this young nation, urged men and women, boys and girls to repent.

The response was overwhelming. Tens of thousands made public confessions of faith up and down the 13 colonies. Benjamin Franklin, a skeptic of the gospel but an admirer of Whitfield, said it seemed as if the whole world were growing religious, so that one could not even walk through the town in an evening without hearing psalms sung by different families on every street. This was what we would call in today's language, revival time.

---

3   The following section is adapted from the video by George Thomas, CBN News, as included in my video "The Third Great Awakening."

What Whitfield and others did was to call people to a personal relationship with Jesus Christ. When they did, the Word of God became the bedrock of society. You had a love for the Scriptures. You had a love for going to church. It became fun to go to church, rather than the old, habitual tradition of attending church.

The gospel also affected other aspects of people's lives. It affected their businesses. It affected their families. It affected every area of life. Historians say no other event of this period helped as much to unite the colonies. The First Great Awakening drew them together in the same common understanding of what society was really all about; of God's call on the nation, of the need to put the gospel into practice.

It also emphasized the truths of the gospel, like individual accountability to God and the idea of self-government under God. America was founded by dissenters. That's what they were called.

The Bible showed the colonists that all were equal in the eyes of God, including the king. While the dark scourge of slavery came to the colonies in 1619, many early American leaders like Franklin and Adams believed that equality was for everyone, black or white, male or female, slave or free. It is out of the Great Awakening that you started seeing the freeing of slaves. People started saying, "Slavery is wrong. I need to let my slaves go."

The First Great Awakening also birthed the strong conviction that government was illegal unless it was rooted in the consent of the governed. All these biblical principles helped lay the foundation for America's political and religious future.

Without religious faith, we would not have had the Revolutionary War, the Declaration of Independence, or the Constitution of the United States. The colonists came out of this period with a sense that America had a spiritual destiny to take the message of democracy and freedom around the globe. The idea spread that we are the light of the world; we're a city set on a hill.

In the end, as the great revival spread through the new land, the colonists were reminded again that life was meaningless without a personal relationship with Jesus Christ. His Word had the power to change the course of history and our nation.

This is the Jonathan Edwards type of preaching that ignited the First Great Awakening. As I mentioned earlier, David Wilkerson spoke to me in 1986. He said, "I see a plague coming on the world. And the bars and the churches and the governments will shut down. The plague will hit New York City and shake it like it has never been shaken. The plague is going to force prayerless believers into radical prayer and into their Bibles. And repentance will be the cry from the men of God in the pulpit. And out of it will spring a Third Great Awakening that will sweep America and the world."

That was 34 years ago. Right now, you are seeing this prophetic revelation begin to be fulfilled. I am sharing with you a prophetic word. There was an anonymous statement that has been moving throughout the internet that the official lockdown started on March 23 in America, and will begin to be lifted on May 1, 40 days later. The Latin root of the word "quarantine" is 40. So what does the Bible say about 40? The flood lasted 40 days. Moses fled Egypt and dwelt in the desert for forty years. For forty days, Moses stayed on Mount Sinai to receive the commandments. The exodus lasted 40 years; Jesus fasted 40 days. The optimum number of weeks for human gestation is 40. One group of theologians thinks that the number 40 represents change. It is a time of preparation where a person or people make a fundamental change.

Something will happen after those 40 days. Just believe and pray. I know what's going to happen. We're going to see the beginning of a Great Awakening. It's coming. It's coming. It's coming! Remember; whenever the number 40 appears in the Bible, there is always a change. Please know that during this quarantine, rivers are cleansing hearts, vegetation is growing, the air is becoming cleaner, and there is less pollution. And most importantly, people are turning to Christ. The Earth is at rest for the first time in my lifetime. And there's a transformation coming. It's called a Great Awakening.

Remember, we are in the year 2020. Twenty plus 20 equals forty. Also, 2020 is the year of the United States census. Jesus Christ, the savior of the world, was born during a census. Lastly, 2020 is perfect vision. May our spiritual sight be on the Lord, to see a Great Awakening, to sense it in our spirit, to yearn for it. May these days, of quarantine bring us out of darkness into spiritual light that will shape the nation and the world.

The parallels between the church prior to the First and Second Great Awakenings and the church today are astonishing. I want to declare to you the steps necessary for a Third Great Awakening.

If we look at the church before the First and Second Great Awakenings, we realize something: The church and the world were very similar. Now, you're going to see this prophetic revelation in a moment in Ezekiel 37. But I'm going to share it in the spirit realm, so may your ears be open.

I want you to think of Ezekiel 37 as God prophesying to the church. Here's what he's saying to you, pastor. In the Book of Revelation, there were seven churches. Five of the seven received a rebuke from God. Five of the seven angels of the churches received a rebuke. These were not physical angels. These "angels" were messengers that represented pastors. Now, think of this as the church:

The hand of the LORD came upon me and brought me out in the Spirit of the LORD, and set me down in the midst of the valley; and it was full of bones. Then He caused me to pass by them all around, and behold, there were very many in the open valley; and indeed they were very dry. And He said to me, "Son of man, can these bones live?"

So I answered, "O Lord GOD, You know" (Ezekiel 37:1-3).

This is prophetically now the message of the Lord and the word of the Lord to the church that has determined it is going to control the Holy Spirit. Some churches act like, "We'll give you an opportunity, Holy Spirit, when you can show up. You can show up sometime in my 20-minute sermon, or our 15 minutes of programmed music, or You can show up when we have our 5-minute altar service."

I'm sorry to tell you, pastor, you're not going to control Him. When the Holy Spirit comes like a river down a mountain, and people try to dam up that river, it breaks through. People who try to build houses on the side of that river are flushed down and the river keeps flowing. Ezekiel continues in verses 4-6:

Again He said to me, "Prophesy to these bones, and say to them, 'O dry bones, hear the word of the LORD! Thus says the Lord GOD to these bones: "Surely I will cause breath to enter into you, and you shall live. I will put sinews on you and bring flesh upon you, cover you with skin and put breath in you; and you shall live. Then you shall know that I *am* the Lord."'"

Do you see that in the spirit realm? They still weren't alive, but he had received the Word of the Lord. I also have a word from the Lord that has burned in me through David Wilkerson's prophecy. As I started seeking the face of God, the Lord gave me revelation into it. Verses 7-8 add:

"So I prophesied as I was commanded; and as I prophesied, there was a noise, and suddenly a rattling; and the bones came together, bone to bone. Indeed, as I looked, the sinews and the flesh came upon them, and the skin covered them over; but *there was* no breath in them."

That reminds me of church leaders who are trying so hard to preach well or to design good worship services. They are trying so hard to please the Lord. But look again at God's conversation with Ezekiel in verses 9-10:

Also He said to me, "Prophesy to the breath, prophesy, son of man, and say to the breath, 'Thus says the Lord God: "Come from the four winds, O breath, and breathe on these slain, that they may live."'" So I prophesied as He commanded me, and breath came into them, and they lived, and stood upon their feet, an exceedingly great army.

This is the church coming alive. It is filled with the power of the Holy Spirit, ablaze for the glory of God because of repentance and intense, radical prayer. Verses 11-14 conclude:

Then He said to me, "Son of man, these bones are the whole house of Israel. They indeed say, 'Our bones are dry, our hope is lost, and we ourselves are cut off!' Therefore prophesy and say to them, 'Thus says the Lord God: "Behold, O My people, I will open your graves and cause you to come up from your graves, and bring you into the land of Israel. Then you shall know that I *am* the Lord, when I have opened your graves, O My people, and brought you up from your graves. I will put My Spirit in you, and you shall live, and I will place you in your own land. Then you shall know that I, the Lord, have spoken *it* and performed *it*," says the Lord.'"

Do you see what the Holy Spirit is saying? The church is going to catch on fire with the glory of God! The pastors are going to catch on fire. The Third Great Awakening is going to be like a resurrection. The bones in the dust are intermingling. They're coming alive.

Man was taken out of the dust to become the people of God. Then Ezekiel saw the people of God had returned to the dust. Man was given dominion over the earth. But now man was buried under the earth. The Word of God was not being proclaimed prophetically, "Thus saith the Lord."

I want to address pastors for a moment. Pastor, when was the last time you stood in the pulpit, trembling under the unction of the Holy Spirit with the prophetic word, declaring, "Thus saith the Lord?" That's what's going to happen in this Third Great Awakening. It's not going to be church as usual, because the spirit of God is going to show up. You don't sit around and have an organized little visitation during a resurrection. You could be at the tomb of Jesus or at the tomb of Lazarus and just say, "We'll program 15 minutes for this section and 10 minutes for that part. . ." That's not how awakening works!

The blood and the cross were being replaced by organized religion and human rationale before the First and Second Great Awakenings. Yet thirsty souls in the desert were being offered cups of water. There was no shortage of bones, but there was an absence of life. Before the Great Awakening, most people in America considered themselves Christians because of their upbringing, their culture, or their spiritual life, but the joy and the power of the Lord were lost. It was a popular religion. However, Scripture declares those who live godly lives in Christ Jesus will suffer persecution. Truly living for the Lord is not comfortable.

Pastor, having a large congregation is not an accurate measure of true transformation. Church activity is simply bones and flesh, noise and rattling, but no spiritual power. The sick are not being healed. The bound are not being set free. A lot of social activity, recreation, and celebration and fleshly energy can be found everywhere. All of this was true in America before the First Great Awakening of 1730 and 1740 and again before the Second Great Awakening between 1790 and 1820.

In the First Great Awakening, God sent men who preached with power, and the church was revived. They helped light a fire that became a revival sweeping across the American colonies. This new personal expression of faith was a powerful change, and it further distanced many of the American people from the Anglican Church, the official state Church of England. With faith becoming separated from government in the minds of many Americans, the seeds of independence would be sown from American church pulpits for the next 30 to 40 years.

As I was preaching one of the messages used in this book, a dear, mighty man of God who leads 61 million believers worldwide for his denomination wrote to me and he said, "Mike, the messages you are preaching are the messages that Jonathan Edwards preached. It's that Jonathan Edwards spirit that could birth a Third Great Awakening." Hallelujah!

During the Second Great Awakening, God sent men who

preached messages of grace and fear; men such as Pastor Charles Finney, who was called the "father of American revivalism." That sounds like the lyrics from a song many believers know: "'Twas grace that taught my heart to fear, and grace my fears relieved."

Today's preaching is on grace, but not on fear. The same characteristics were in five of the seven churches in Revelation that the Lord rebuked. They were churches of grace without fear. What were they promising? They promised a blessed life. "Come to my church, pay your tithes and you'll have a blessed life. Give a double tithe; you'll have a doubly-blessed life." I challenge you to find this in the book of Acts, or find it in the life of Jesus or the apostle Peter or John or Paul, or in the early church.

Life wasn't about them and it wasn't about a blessed life. It was about surrendering their lives, giving their lives to the Lord Jesus Christ to shake and transform our world.

What is necessary for a Great Awakening to come to your church and to America and the world? There must be a call from the church to come out and rise up from the world's system. We must shake off these dry bones from the dust of the earth and rise up in our place as servants of the Lord to the world. We can no longer continue to be enamored by a culture that wants us to compromise and be like them for acceptance.

Can you hear it? "Come out from among them And be separate,

says the Lord. Do not touch what is unclean, And I will receive you" (2 Corinthians 6:17). The Word must be proclaimed against those who refuse to preach the power of the Holy Spirit.

Trust me; it will interrupt your worship service. It will be a divine interruption. God is getting ready to move like He's never moved. Soon, we're going to see a Great Awakening, a mighty manifestation. There needs to be a return to the pulpits, of hungry and thirsty prophetic words from pastors raised from the dead to life again. Not itching ears and entertaining people, but declaring the Word of the Lord and bringing conviction of the soul as did Jonathan Edwards.

In 2 Timothy 4:3-4 we are told, "For the time will come when they will not endure sound doctrine, but according to their own desires, *because* they have itching ears, they will heap up for themselves teachers; and they will turn *their* ears away from the truth, and be turned aside to fables." We need to stop celebrating the number of the bones in the room and start calling the dead to life. Crowds can serve as the mark of popularity of an event more than the conviction of the heart. Remember the words of Jesus in Matthew 7:22-23:

> "Many will say to Me in that day, 'Lord, Lord, have we not prophesied in Your name, cast out demons in Your name, and done many wonders in Your name?' And then I will declare to them, 'I never knew you; depart from Me, you who practice lawlessness!'"

Matthew 24:33 adds, "When you see these things happening, recognize that he is near, even at the door."

When I was visiting President Ronald Reagan in the Oval Office, he showed me his mother's Bible. It had been opened to Romans 8:22: "For we know that the whole creation groans and labors with birth pangs together until now." His mother had written next to these words, "Son, this Scripture is for the healing of the nation." I saw her very handwriting.

Then there are the famous revival words of 2 Chronicles 7:13-14:

> "When I shut up heaven and there is no rain, or command the locusts to devour the land, or send pestilence among My people, if My people who are called by My name will humble themselves, and pray and seek My face, and turn from their wicked ways, then I will hear from heaven, and will forgive their sin and heal their land."

You may think, "We're God's people, right?" But God says we are wicked. If you don't know you're wicked, it's even worse. It means you have a stone-cold heart. Isaiah the prophet quickly discovered his wickedness when he experienced the presence of God Almighty. He cried out, "Woe is me, for I am unclean" (Isaiah 6:5). You cannot feel comfortable in the presence of God. That's what a Third Great Awakening is going to do.

Here's a sermon from Peter, the rock and leader of the apostles: The core of the message of the book of Acts declares, "Repent therefore and be converted, that your sins may be blotted out, so that times of refreshing may come from the presence of the Lord" (Acts 3:19, NKJV). It is repentance that will usher in an outpouring of the Holy Spirit and a Third Great Awakening. I believe this Great Awakening will usher in the fulfillment of that prophecy.

In Matthew 21:13, Jesus taught, "'My house shall be called a house of prayer,' but you have made it a 'den of thieves.'" If Jesus came into your church, what would he do? Would he stand up before your congregation and say, "Good job, you've become a house of prayer"? How much prayer is going on in your church? A little prayer at the beginning or end of your service is not sufficient. That's not a house of prayer. That's organized religion.

There's going to be a move of God where people are going to show up before the service begins. They're going to be in the front of your church, flat on their face, crying out to God in repentance. When you see that, you will know it is the beginning of a Great Awakening.

The Third Great Awakening is beginning. God will set us free from the dominion of sin, not by strengthening our old, religious man, but by crucifying him. It's all about the cross.

The Third Great Awakening will smash the idols of control. I hear the voice of John the Baptist from Matthew 3:10: "And even now the ax is laid to the root of the trees. Therefore every tree which does not bear good fruit is cut down and thrown into the fire."

What is good fruit? Good fruit honors the glory of God that brings resurrection to the dry bones. Hallelujah! Believers will come out of their prayer closets, having repented and cried, rushing into their churches, falling flat on their faces for hours. Churches will be flooded with hundreds and thousands of interceding souls. As 2 Corinthians 6:17-18 says, they will be souls that "come out from among them." They will be cleansed by the power of the Holy Spirit, sons and daughters on fire for the glory of the Lord.

Let me repeat to you a short message on holiness: "Do not love the world or the things in the world. If anyone loves the world, the love of the Father is not in him. For all that is in the world—the lust of the flesh, the lust of the eyes, and the pride of life—is not of the Father but is of the world" (1 John 2:15-16). I said the second sign of a Great Awakening will be repentant pastors. The apostle John said in 1 John 2:18, "Little children, it is the last hour; and as you have heard that the Antichrist is coming, even now many antichrists have come, by which we know that it is the last hour."

There is a Christ on the throne of your life: It will either be the Lord Jesus Christ or the spirit of lawlessness, the Antichrist. I'll tell you how you can know. When flesh is on the throne of your life, chaos will be the norm, and you will be at peace with your sins. The sins that convicted you when you first came to Christ won't convict you anymore. You're hardhearted.

Isaiah 30:1-2 declares:

> "Woe to the rebellious children," says the LORD,
>
> "Who take counsel, but not of Me,
>
> And who devise plans, but not of My Spirit,
>
> That they may add sin to sin;
>
> Who walk to go down to Egypt,
>
> And have not asked My advice,
>
> To strengthen themselves in the strength of Pharaoh,
>
> And to trust in the shadow of Egypt!"

We need to stop building congregations of flesh and start building armies of the Spirit where there is noise and the rattling instead of superficial substitutes. No more substitutes except the breath of God and a church empowered by the Holy Ghost. The call of the man of God and the people of God are not about you. It's not about your blessed life. It's about dying to everything and letting Christ make you a flame of fire for a lost and dying world, no matter the cost.

I am praying that the Holy Spirit will open your eyes as you read the words of this chapter. I pray you will become part of this Third Great Awakening. May God make the truth of His amazing grace afresh in your life today as we conclude this chapter with the powerful words of the classic hymn:

"Amazing Grace, how sweet the sound

That saved a wretch like me

I once was lost, but now am found

Was blind but now I see

Was Grace that taught my heart to fear

And Grace, my fears relieved

How precious did that Grace appear

The hour I first believed."

QUESTIONS FOR DISCUSSION

✧ What does it mean to humble ourselves before the Lord? How can we do this individually? As a church?

✧ Do you believe God is sending a Third Great Awakening? What are you doing to prepare to serve in part of God's plan of revival?

✧ Why do you think God has waited so long to send another awakening to America? How do you believe a coming awakening will transform people, churches, and society?

✧ In what ways could you see God use you in the Third Great Awakening? Consider you talents and abilities as possible ways to serve the Lord today and in the days ahead to impact lives for eternity.

IMITATION ALTARS

In both 2 Kings 16 and 2 Chronicles 28, we find God's people were experiencing a period of decline because of their idolatry. Idolatry is anything that comes between you and God. Isaiah 40:6-7 says it this way:

> The voice said, "Cry out!"
> And he said, "What shall I cry?"
> "All flesh *is* grass,
> And all its loveliness *is* like the flower of the field.
> The grass withers, the flower fades,
> Because the breath of the LORD blows upon it;
> Surely the people *are* grass."

Everything that issues from the flesh, even religious flesh, is grass. As with the flowers of the field, the grass withers and the flowers fade. It's like the Holy Spirit was saying, "I want you to understand that religious flesh is like grass. It fits into the realm of the temporal. It fits into the realm of the passing away. This isn't some flesh; it's all flesh. Yes, even religious flesh."

I want to explain this for a moment. Maybe you're thinking, "I'm a believer and I love God." That may be true, but you also may be very content in your faith. It's not risky anymore. It's comfortable, convenient, and controlled. God may want to interrupt it because all flesh has a tendency to focus on being temporal, shallow, fragile, and fickle.

There is another quality to grass. Grass is prolific. There's a lot of it. In our lives, flesh has that same kind of quality. There is fragility and shallowness about the nature of flesh. Our mind can be easily distracted. Our emotions can be so easily stirred up and manipulated that nothing really matters. We think we've arrived. Our will can be hard to bend to the ways of the Holy Spirit. Our natural senses are very central and can be easily distracted in those areas. It's just like grass.

God says this about the flesh: Grass is beautiful, but it can also be deceptive. When I first began serving in the ministry, I filmed a television special in Jerusalem. I had a camera crew with me and we drove out to do some filming. We had all the equipment in the van.

There was a Muslim man right by the van who was praying. When we came back from filming, I turned to my producer and said, "Hey, he robbed us. He stole everything!"

The man was religious in praying, but he had also stolen our equipment. The producer smiled and said, "Yeah, and he got his prayers answered." The man may have appeared to be devout, but his actions revealed his true intentions.

We are not as different from that man as you might think. Rather than repenting and returning to the covenant with heaven, the people of God in the Old Testament rebelled and sought a contract with the world. The same takes place still today. The church has modeled itself after the world. God says that all of its loveliness is like the flower, or a field of flowers. Flowers are beautiful! The problem is not the beauty of the flower; the problem is that it withers. It does not last. There's something temporal about the flesh,; it's not something you can build a life upon.

You can't build a life upon human intellect. You can't build a life upon emotions or your desires or your personal pride and your religion. You can't build a life upon your sensuality. We can become so focused on the physical realm, yet this will fade and wither. The flesh profits nothing. A lot can be done in our lives in the flesh. We can generate much activity, but it profits nothing.

No flesh, not even religious flesh, can glory in the presence of the Lord. What originates out of the flesh, out of our emotions, out of our will, out of our sensuality, cannot in the end satisfy as much as the presence of the Lord. The Bible talks about two brothers, Ishmael and Isaac. One was called the child of the flesh; the other, the child of promise. The blessing was based on the connection with the Lord. The Bible says that the flesh is not just different than the Spirit, but the flesh is the opposite of the Spirit. It's contrary to the Spirit.

The people of God robbed the treasury of the temple to purchase a pagan partnership. They exchanged their reliance on God for an alliance with the world. Paul the apostle, writing in Roman 7 regarding the flesh, said, "I know that within me (in this flesh) there dwelled no good thing." The flesh cannot glory in the presence of God. The flesh doesn't profit anything. In the end, the flesh persecutes the life of the Spirit and the flesh. Paul tells us there's no good thing that dwells in the flesh.

My passion and my flesh, he says, are incorrigible. That doesn't mean that I'm irredeemable, because the Bible says that I've been born again by an incorruptible seed. When I accept Christ and am born of the Spirit, I receive an incorruptible seed. That seed is at war against the flesh, but my spirit is incorruptible.

My flesh is corruptible, so in my flesh dwells no good thing. An incorruptible seed has been planted on the inside of me. There's a reason why the flesh withers and the flower fades in our lives. There's something that must happen with this incorrigible flesh. We desire to be accepted by the world, and this desire has become more important than being faithful to God.

What is it that must happen? As verse seven says, the grass withers and the flower fades. Why? The breath of the Lord blows upon it. In other words, the picture here is that the Lord causes the flesh to wither. What causes the loveliness of our flesh and our eyes to fade is when the breath of the Lord breathes on them. The breath of the Lord causes the flowers to fade, and the loveliness that we hold in our flesh begins to wither.

There's a withering power to the breath of God. This is a powerful revelation to me. I believe the Lord is yearning to transform religious flesh. He wants us to lift our lives above the level of religious flesh. In normal circumstances, our flesh is pretty and prolific, but if the truth is told, there's a lot of stuff that feeds our flesh in our churches. There's a lot of stuff that fertilizes and nurtures our flesh. There is so much activity, so much appeal to our emotions. We hear too much that agrees with our nature and our will, too much which appeal to our sinful nature. Our flesh is being nourished instead of fading away.

Our flesh is being fed a lot in our normal everyday experience. As a believer, we're proud of our flesh. Maybe for some of us, some of it is flesh that's nauseous in the nostrils of God, even though it's religious flesh. My favorite poem is by John Steinbeck. It's called "The Dangerous Difference," and reads:

"After a while you'll think no thought the others do not think. You'll know no word the others can't say. And you'll do things because the others do them. You'll feel the danger in any difference whatever-a danger to the crowd of like-thinking, like-acting men. . . Once in a while there is a man who won't do what is demanded of him, and do you know what happens? The whole machine devotes itself coldly to the destruction of his difference. They'll beat your spirit and your nerves, your body and your mind, with iron rods until the dangerous difference goes out of you. And if you can't finally give in, they'll vomit you up and leave you stinking outside—neither part of themselves, nor yet free. . .They only do it to protect themselves. A thing so triumphantly illogical, so beautifully senseless as an army can't allow a question to weaken it."

That's the dilemma you face as a believer in the house of the Lord. That which God had designed was pushed aside for that which the culture preferred. Have you been crossing the line where you have been violating God's clear Holy spirit conviction? Maybe you've been captivated by your activity and your emotions and the applause of man. So many things are drawing your attention, and your religious flesh is flourishing.

The problem with all flesh flourishing is that all flesh profits nothing, including religious flesh. Our flesh will never be able to glory in the presence of God. Our flesh is never going to be able to be declared to be incorruptible. Our flesh is incorrigible. I know within me there dwells no good thing, so what value is it for me to allow my flesh to flourish and be nourished all the time?

My spirit, which is incorruptible and has been changed by Christ, is unable to grow in the fullness of what God wants to do. How can I come into agreement with the Lord's desire for my flesh to fade and for the flower and the beauty of that flesh to wither? The breath of the Lord must blow on our flesh. That's what causes the grass to weather and the flower to fade; when the breath of the Lord blows upon it.

The Holy Spirit has shown me that a Great Awakening is coming. He revealed this to me in my prayer room after several weeks of agonizing and repenting and humbling myself and going back to my first love and saying, "God, whatever the cost, I'll do it. I'll declare the Word of the Lord." God is going to bring a Great Awakening, but here's how it's going to happen: You're going to have to repent. You will be required to humble yourself and see yourself the way I saw myself.

Isaiah said, "Woe is me. I am unclean." Get the spotlight off yourself and see a holy God in that pulpit, Pastor. The Lord said to me that believers are going to be moved by the Spirit to flood their churches even before the services start. They will fall flat on their faces at the altars, crying out to God in repentance. Those will be the first two signs of the Great Awakening.

What does it mean to have the Lord breathe upon your flesh? When we look at John 20, the Bible says that Jesus, after he was resurrected from the dead, appeared to His disciples, and according to John 20:22 He breathed on them. Jesus said, "Receive the Holy Spirit." Breathing the breath of God upon them was the very first thing Jesus did when He gathered His disciples in the place where He would reveal Himself as having been resurrected from the dead. The first thing He wants to do in your church, Pastor, is to breathe on you and your congregation.

Jesus does not need your worship, your preaching, or your commercials. The breath of God is waiting on the Holy Spirit for divine visitation. Why did Jesus want to breathe on them? Because the breath of the Lord withers our outer man and releases a new incorruptible life inside you. It's interesting what the Bible says about the Word of God. It says that all Scripture is given by inspiration of God and is profitable for doctrine, for reproof, correction, instruction, and righteousness (2 Timothy 3:16-17). The word *theopneustos* in the Greek language has to do with the breath of God.

What is the Spirit of the Lord saying to us? During the time of isolation, when you've been alone, how much of the breath of God, the Spirit of God, and the Word of God has saturated your soul? How many of your hours did you spend in front of your television listening to the news or tormenting your emotions with fear and panic? How much did we feed our sensual flesh? Or did we allow the Spirit of God to resurrect us during this season? This was an unprecedented opportunity to come out of your grave.

I don't know if there will ever be another time in our lives when we will have a greater opportunity to truly let God begin to breathe on us. The grass withers and the flowers fade, but the Word of the Lord and the Spirit of God can have access to our lives in transforming power. The flesh is demanding Lordship. It cries out loudly in our lives. If we allow God to breathe on our flesh, "self" will begin to fade. The flower and the loveliness we valued so highly in our pride will begin to perish.

In the Spirit, the incorruptible seed, the inner life of Christ will change us. There will be a greater sensitivity to the Holy Spirit, a greater sense of urgency to the presence of the power of Christ. I believe you may be discovering this now. God is revealing sins that you weren't convicted of the last few years which bothered you when you became a new believer. They're losing their grip on you. Your heart is softening. You're getting hungry for the breath of God, a real move of the Holy spirit, the presence and the power of God.

There's a lot of "word" going out right now. So many things are being discussed; so many sermons, so much information. We are bombarded with extremes daily. But is it transforming the world?

Is it shaking the world like the day of Pentecost? Are signs and wonders happening? Are the sick really being healed? Is the glory of God really falling? If not, then the breath of God is not there.

The flesh wants to ascend to the throne of your life and make you believe that you are in a very special place with God and you can glory in all your idols. Some are making your church your idol or your pastor your idol. That's how you see God. You're living vicariously through a person or place. I hope the Scripture has revealed something to you concerning this matter.

We must seek that which is in touch with heaven rather than that which is pleasing the world and becoming like the world. When Jesus breathed on his disciples, what was He breathing? Who was Jesus? He was God clothed in human flesh, incarnate, raised from the dead, and the first thing He wanted to do was breathe on his disciples.

This is a Holy Spirit led message. I've been with Jesus. I see what God wants to bring: a manifestation of His glory like the world has never seen, but we must get out of the way. We're all going to have to humble ourselves. No one can glory in His presence. Let your prayer be, "Holy Father, let your Spirit open my heart to the mighty wind, so there can be a sweet, sweet spirit in this place."

When I first came to the Lord and attended Bible college, I used to go into the prayer room for sometimes four, five, six hours, and it seemed like only minutes because I was caught up in the Lord. I had a breakthrough. I was in His presence. Nothing was affecting me. The awakening is coming! You're either going to be a part of it, or you're going to be pushed aside as a goat. I pray to God that you'll hear and receive the word of the Lord.

QUESTIONS FOR DISCUSSION

✧ What does it mean to have an imitation altar? What are some of the imitation altars that compete for our attention today?

✧ When was a time you have sensed God powerfully at work in your prayers? What would it take to see God work in such ways through your prayers more frequently?

✧ How would you desire to have God spiritually refresh you and "breathe" into your life in a new way?

✧ God would like to work through you to help others. As you consider others in your life, who is someone God is leading you to encourage in their walk with the Lord?

I SAW THE LORD

en's thrones are removed, so that's God's thrones will be raised. Isaiah 6:1 reads, "In the year that King Uzziah died, I saw the Lord sitting on a throne, high and lifted up, and the train of His robe filled the temple." I want to ask you a question: When was the last time you saw the Lord? When was the last time His glory filled your heart and your life? I'm not talking about emotions. I'm not talking about inspiration. I'm talking about the power of the presence of God that overtook you like a tornado.

Tragedy always produces a response. It's either repentance or rebellion, and we're in the midst of tragedy. In the 1960s, three American leaders were killed—Robert Kennedy, John Kennedy, and Martin Luther King, Jr. When they died, there was a response. It was rebellion and repentance at the same time.

Out of the 1960s came rebellion and the "God is dead" movement, LSD, drugs, and sexual promiscuity. Yet, also out of those years came the Jesus movement, where hundreds of thousands of young people came to Christ.

Let me share my own personal experience with death and what I saw, because I did see the Lord. I described this account in the introduction, but want to include some additional details here, as well.

My father was a Jew hater, but he married a Jewish woman. She never knew it until many years later. He ended up claiming I was not his son, arguing she had an affair with a Jewish man. He abused me violently. At the age of 11 he was beating my mother up one night and I tried to protect her at 1:30 in the morning, screaming, "Stop it!" He ran up the stairs, picked me up by my throat above his head, and strangled me. I remember looking into those drunk, bloodshot eyes and thinking, "I'm dead. It's over."

I passed out, and later awoke gagging. I had vomited all over myself. I was in a fetal position, angry and screaming at God. I shouted, "Why was I born?" It made no sense. This man never called me son. He never said he loved me and never affirmed me. My mother was being beaten every Friday night because of me. I didn't believe in God. I didn't believe in Jesus. The only Jesus I saw was my father.

But moments later, the room became bright like I've never before experienced. In the midst of the brightness, I saw two hands coming toward me. Nail scars were in the wrists. Then I raised my head and saw the eyes. Every color of the rainbow was in those eyes. They were like magnets. They were smiling eyes, and then He spoke.

The first thing He said was: "Son." No one had ever called me son. The second thing He said was, "I love you." I had never heard those words from my father. Then He said something that really astonished me. He said, "I have a great plan for your life." I had seen the Lord, and was radically transformed by the glory of God. In Isaiah 6:2-6 (NKJV) we read:

> "Above it stood seraphim; each one had six wings: with two he covered his face, with two he covered his feet, and with two he flew. And one cried to another and said:

> "Holy, holy, holy *is* the LORD of hosts;
> The whole earth *is* full of His glory!"

> And the posts of the door were shaken by the voice of him who cried out, and the house was filled with smoke.

> So I said:
> "Woe *is* me, for I am undone!
> Because I *am* a man of unclean lips,
> And I dwell in the midst of a people of unclean lips;

For my eyes have seen the King,

The LORD of hosts."

God's glory will be revealed. I don't think any believers are shouting now that the whole earth is full of His glory. Only the Spirit of the Lord can reveal that to you. You look and you become frightened and panicked and obsessed with the news, rather than seeing through the eyes of the Spirit.

Let me tell you about a long-ago conversation in a cave. The cave is called Jeremiah's Cave or Jeremiah's Grotto. Jeremiah was left behind in a desolate city after all the Babylonian captives were taken. How did it happen that a city once full of people, full of kings and queens and the glory of God, now was desolate and empty? There was no sound of people calling in its streets. There were neither songs of joy, nor anything of value. all valuables now rested in the homes of others.

You could look at the city and ask, "Where was the glory of the temple? Where were the people rejoicing and worshiping? How did these great men and women disappear? Where was this great city, Jerusalem? How did it fail to maintain its greatness and fall short of its destiny?" All the prophets, priests, and kings had prophesied there. In his early ministry, Jeremiah was primarily a preaching prophet, and was not very popular. As a matter of fact, neither was David Wilkerson. My wife and I started Teen Challenge in Arkansas two months after we were married; that was the ministry founded by Wilkerson.

I loved Brother Dave. He preached a strong message of repentance, and many preachers wouldn't come to his meetings. They didn't receive it. They rejected his message just as Jeremiah was rejected. Jeremiah cried out against idolatry. Brother Dave did that, too. Jeremiah cried out against the greed of the priests and false prophets. The chief overseer of the temple heard of it and had Jeremiah beaten and placed in stocks.

Stocks were an instrument of torture in that day in which the body was forced into unnatural positions, confining the arms, legs, and head by means of wooden beams that locked into place. Understandably, Jeremiah became discouraged. We read in Jeremiah 20:14-18 that he cried out in the darkness:

"Cursed *be* the day in which I was born!
Let the day not be blessed in which my mother bore me!
Let the man *be* cursed
Who brought news to my father, saying,
"A male child has been born to you!"
Making him very glad.
And let that man be like the cities
Which the LORD overthrew, and did not relent;
Let him hear the cry in the morning

And the shouting at noon,

Because he did not kill me from the womb,

That my mother might have been my grave,

And her womb always enlarged *with me*.

Why did I come forth from the womb to see labor and sorrow,

That my days should be consumed with shame?"

I believe I know how Jeremiah felt. I felt the same way when my father strangled me. Jeremiah was discouraged because he was a man standing against a flood of filth, and "pickpocket priesthood." No one who is fighting the spiritual battle in our generation can sleep on a comfortable mattress and preach a gospel that says, "God loves you just the way you are. Everything's just fine. You don't have to worry. You've got a guarantee. There's no price to pay. There are no sacrifices to make."

In Jeremiah 24, Jeremiah was given a vision: two baskets of figs. One basket had very good figs, but the other was filled with bad figs. And the Lord asked in verse 3: "What do you see, Jeremiah?" Jeremiah didn't understand what God was showing him at first. People were dying, the city had been attacked, but God was talking about figs? It didn't make sense.

Jeremiah answered, "Figs, the good figs, very good; and the bad, very bad, which cannot be eaten, they are so bad" (v. 3b). God had an explanation for him in verses 4-7:

Again the word of the LORD came to me, saying, "Thus says the LORD, the God of Israel: 'Like these good figs, so will I acknowledge those who are carried away captive from Judah, whom I have sent out of this place for *their own* good, into the land of the Chaldeans. For I will set My eyes on them for good, and I will bring them back to this land; I will build them and not pull *them* down, and I will plant them and not pluck *them* up. Then I will give them a heart to know Me, that I *am* the LORD; and they shall be My people, and I will be their God, for they shall return to Me with their whole heart.'"

Jeremiah had several contemporaries, who shared a positive message, yet Jeremiah only saw the darkness and he lamented that darkness. Then God gave him light. Jeremiah began his ministry as a young man during the reign of King Josiah. When others were taken into captivity, Jeremiah was forced into Egypt and his ministry was restricted in that group. Daniel, if you'll recall, was one of the young men that was taken to the king's court in Babylon and eventually rose to the highest level of government. As for Ezekiel, he was taken to the rivers of Babylon as a slave laborer. He and his fellow captives dug and maintained the canals branching off to the Euphrates River. This was several miles from Babylon itself. Each of these men was a prophet, but they had specific ministries to specific groups of people.

It doesn't appear that they came in contact with each other, though the book of Daniel tells us he was aware of his people down by the river and had a great concern and compassion for them. We don't have any clear indication that Daniel knew Jeremiah, yet his writing shows us Daniel was aware of Jeremiah's prophecies.

Let me tell you where the cave of Jeremiah was. The cave where the conversation took place between Jeremiah and God was near Jerusalem. When I visited Jerusalem, Mayor Teddy Kollek, knew I liked the book of Jeremiah and asked, "Would you like to visit Jeremiah's cave?" He took me to it. The cave of Jeremiah has a different name today, Golgotha.

The assignment that God gave this prophet was going to be at the spot where the blood of the Lamb flowed from Calvary. Think of it, he ended up with a divine appointment with destiny that was so much greater than he thought. When you have truly been with Jesus, there's only one response: I am unclean.

When God's glory is revealed, man's pride is done. What does this mean for the church today? In many cases, the church exists, but it's not prevailing against the gates of hell. In Ezekiel's vision of the valley of dry bones, we read in Ezekiel 37:1-8:

> The hand of the LORD came upon me and brought me out in the Spirit of the LORD, and set me down in the midst of the valley; and it *was* full of bones. Then He

caused me to pass by them all around, and behold, there were very many in the open valley; and indeed they were very dry. And He said to me, "Son of man, can these bones live?"

So I answered, "O Lord GOD, You know."

Again He said to me, "Prophesy to these bones, and say to them, 'O dry bones, hear the word of the LORD! Thus says the Lord GOD to these bones: "Surely I will cause breath to enter into you, and you shall live. I will put sinews on you and bring flesh upon you, cover you with skin and put breath in you; and you shall live. Then you shall know that I am the LORD."'"

So I prophesied as I was commanded; and as I prophesied, there was a noise, and suddenly a rattling; and the bones came together, bone to bone. Indeed, as I looked, the sinews and the flesh came upon them, and the skin covered them over; but there was no breath in them.

God has not forsaken the church, but the church is not a building. It's the body of Christ. If you focus on it as a building, you will rob God's glory. You'll be so distracted with the physical realm that you won't even see the glory of God. God is the one who attached tendons to you, made flesh come upon you, and covered you with skin. He is the one who breathed life into you so you will know He is the Lord.

I want to ask you a question: Why are five of the seven churches in the book of Revelation rebuked by God? You have a church that loves God, loves his Word, but then you have the church at Ephesus. It had abandoned its first love for Christ. It was a compromised church. The church at Sardis was called spiritually dead. The seventh church, the church of Laodicea, was called lukewarm. It was neither cold nor hot toward God. Jesus said He would spew it out of His mouth. Jesus wasn't rebuking angels, these angels or "messengers" were pastors of the seven churches.

Looking again at Ezekiel 37:9-10, the Lord adds these words:

> Also He said to me, "Prophesy to the breath, prophesy, son of man, and say to the breath, 'Thus says the Lord GOD: "Come from the four winds, O breath, and breathe on these slain, that they may live."'" So I prophesied as He commanded me, and breath came into them, and they lived, and stood upon their feet, an exceedingly great army.

This was a revived church, a church that had been totally delivered from all idols. God is a holy God and He cannot work through unprepared, unholy vessels. He won't put dirty dishes on the table to feed the world. He's holy. We must also be holy. You cannot be holy until you're in the presence of a holy God. We are called to be a church on its face before a holy God in repentance, a church that has seen the Lord, a church with a pastor with a broken heart in the pulpit who is trembling. That is what is going to change the world. This is a wonderful promise that God has given us. It's a promise to the church to be a glorious church, to be a powerful church, to be an anointed church. Don't settle for anything but the presence of the power of God.

Grace only comes to the humble. There are no superstars in the body of Christ. No celebrities, no need for autographs. Man's pride is undone, so that man's calling will be restored. Do you remember when the fire of God was on you so strongly that you didn't care what anybody thought, and people wondered what had happened to you? Remember the passion you once had for Jesus? We must fix our eyes on Jesus, because there's a world crying out in pain that needs a resurrection. Only a resurrected church can produce resurrecting power.

The proof that grace has come will be when you no longer think of yourself; it's not all about you. It's not about your passion or your purposes or your prosperity. Christian missionary Jim Elliot, who gave his life in Ecuador for the Gospel said, "A man is no fool when he gives what he cannot keep to gain what he cannot lose." The Spirit of God has dealt with me so strongly about this message. Only the

Holy Spirit can open your eyes to understand what I'm saying. I'm not condemning pastors. I love those who lead the church. I know a lot of them are hurting. They are rejected and wounded and try to protect themselves from all the pain. They're afraid to admit that they're not perfect for the pulpit, because they don't want to be rejected and hurt again. Pastor, it's not about us. It's about Him and our brothers and sisters. If you see Jesus, if you see His glory, you'll cry out in tears, "I'm unclean. I'm undone!" When you get to that point is when the glory of God will transform you, your church, your city, and the world.

When Nehemiah saw the condition of Jerusalem, the Bible says that he sat down and wept and mourned and fasted and prayed before the God of heaven. This is going to be a sign of the Third Great Awakening. There's going to be godly repentance, because much of the church today is married to the world.

The church has become lukewarm. There is no brokenness in the pulpits or the fear of God. Sinners are not being convicted of their sins. Daniel cried out, "We have sinned and committed iniquity and have done wickedly" (Daniel 9:5). You can't possibly be in the presence of a holy God and not fall on your face in repentance and with anguish.

We need God's messengers to speak the truth and lead this nation into this next great revival without compromise and without fear. It's coming! It's coming! It's coming!

212

QUESTIONS FOR DISCUSSION

✧ When Isaiah saw the Lord's presence, he recognized his sinfulness before Him and responded in humility. What are some ways you may need to humble yourself to better serve the Lord?

✧ Isaiah said, "Here am I. Send me," when the Lord called for him. As you seek the Lord in prayer, in what ways is God calling you to be sent out and serve Him?

✧ Do you feel like many churches are weak in their impact today? If so, what do you see as the barriers from God working more powerfully in today's churches or in your church?

✧ We are to deal with the sins in our own life, but God also sometimes uses us to address the weakness in the lives of others. Is there someone God is leading you to pray for and provide assistance in turning to the Lord or returning to Him? Pray for an opportunity to help as the Lord allows.

TAKE OFF YOUR CROWNS

Israel was in a season where they were being challenged and tested. It was a season of judgment, and it had to do with Babylon and the city of Jerusalem and enemies and a raid. During this context of testing, there was a specific thing that the Lord commanded the people of God to do. Ezekiel 21:26-27 shares:

> "Thus, says the Lord God, remove the turban and take off the crown. Nothing shall remain the same. Exalt the humble and humble the exalted. Overthrown, overthrown, I will make it overthrown! It shall be no longer until he comes whose right it is, and I will give it to him."

The Lord wants to work in the church in a big way to change our world. However, the work starts in the church. God begins by talking

215

about human kingdoms coming down. Notice what He says: "remove the turban and take off the crown."

When I read that, my first thought was of the word "dethroning." However, the Lord took me to a different word. This is not dethroning; this is abdication. He is saying, "I want you to remove the turban. I want you to take off the crown. I want your kingdom. The things you've been building, your dreams, your focus, your intentions. I want the crown. I want you to abdicate your throne. I want you (speaking to me and to you) to step down off your throne."

When we get to the place where we accept the Word of God as it really is, we remove that crown, and remove that sense of prestige and power. We loosen the turban and set it aside. Then we begin to understand the meaning of, "I've seen your ministry. Now I want to show you mine." So much of what we do is what I call intrinsically myopic. We see everything through our own eyes. That's not how the Holy Spirit works.

Let me give you an example of what happens when you have a divine visitation: God spoke to me many years ago during the Persian Gulf War to go to Iraq. I travelled there through the land of the Kurds. When I arrived, there was a crisis taking place. Saddam Hussein was trying to gas the Kurds.

I was alone as I drove through Turkey into Kurdistan. I had brought medicine, food, and blankets. I worked with Doctors

Without Borders, and preached through a Kurdish interpreter. While preaching one day, I felt the Lord saying, "Preach on Jonah and Nineveh."

That didn't make any sense to me. I thought the Kurds probably didn't know a thing about Jonah and Nineveh, but I obeyed the Lord. When I finished, I gave an altar call. Only one old man came to the Lord.

I was a little discouraged and thought, "I messed up on that message." But my Kurdish interpreter was leaping with joy! I said, "But just one person came to the Lord."

He answered, "You don't know who he is, do you? He's the Sheik of Nineveh. You preached on Nineveh, and the people repented. He just did!"

Because of that man coming to the Lord, I received a state invitation to visit Kurdistan from President Nechirvan Barzani. I took my son Michael with me. We stayed in the Vice President's palace. It was astonishing. They lined up at the airport when we arrived to salute us and welcome us.

When you take off your crown, your plans, your dreams, and your visions, then you can dethrone everything in your life and let His kingdom come, and His will be done. Do you get that? I know it's hard. How do I know this? Because the Bible says the kingdoms of this world are going to become the kingdoms of our Lord and of His Christ.

There's only one way this can happen. There must be a dethroning. I know that's tough for you, because as a believer you're thinking, "Well, everything we do is of the Lord." No, it's not. Everything you do is not of the Lord. Not everything. Some of it is of the Lord; some of it is not.

God is speaking to us in these words. He's not speaking to the world; He's speaking to the church, the body of Christ, and saying, "I want you to dethrone self. I want you to abdicate. I want you to lay down your crown and remove your turban. I'm asking you to do this work. The things that you've been building and dreaming of and focusing your passion, plans, and purposes on, I want you to lay down. I want you to take the crown off your head."

That crown happens to represent the things in which you take pride. On one hand, I'm very proud of my ministry. I'm proud of what we're doing in Jerusalem with the Friends of Zion Heritage Center, and the Ten Boom work in Holland. But the Lord has spoken to me, saying, "There's something more important than even what you're doing; It's what I am doing." Can you lay it all down? That's tough!

This picture is so powerful to me because this is a season that we've never before experienced. It's a historic time, a time of testing in our world. Something is also happening in the church. During the COVID-19 pandemic, churches closed. I heard people say, "We're not going to church."

Oh, yes, you are. The church is not a building; it's the body of Christ. Take off your crown. If you don't, God will take it off for you, and expose you. Remember the Scripture: "Be sure your sin will find you out" (Numbers 32:23).

The apostle John saw the elders bow at the feet of Jesus. In their words of worship, they indicated that despite what they had done on earth to earn their crown, only Jesus was worthy of glory and honor. In the presence of the Lord, all the good deeds we have done will pale by comparison. A crown will seem insignificant to us in the presence of a holy God who gave His life for us (Revelation 2:20).

In today's church, many leaders have begun to build and defend their own kingdoms. There are individuals ascending to the throne, having positions of power and authority. It's a very dangerous thing.

The vision becomes a dream. The dream becomes an organization. The organization becomes a monument. Then, too many worship it. It becomes an 800-pound tail wagging a dog. Our own rule and realm isn't what God wants. The Lord is saying to us, "Take off your crown. I want you to abdicate your throne." Isaiah 6:2-4 reads:

Above it stood seraphim; each one had six wings: with two he covered his face, with two he covered his feet, and with two he flew. And one cried to another and said:

"Holy, holy, holy *is* the LORD of hosts;

The whole earth *is* full of His glory!"

And the posts of the door were shaken by the voice

of him who cried out, and the house was filled with

smoke.

These words deeply impact me. In Hebrew it's, *kadosh, kadosh, kadosh,* "Holy, holy, holy is the Lord." It's a powerful revelation. God doesn't want us to one day rule ourselves. He chooses to rule and reign. The Bible says we're in Christ. He is our light who shall appear. When He appears in His fullness, then we will also appear with Him in glory (Colossians 3:4).

Our rule and reign are attached inseparably to Christ's. When we ascend to our own throne, when we build our own religious kingdoms, when we hold on to our own rule and reign, we're diminishing what God desires to do in our lives.

The Lord is asking pastors and all believers to take off the crowns. If you follow my ministry, or you're a fan of any pastor's ministry, you can become so enamored with the person and their work that you lose your focus on the One for whom they work.

Many have built their own kingdoms. They have constructed their own spiritual façade. Take off the turban. Lift off the crown. Hear *kadosh, kadosh, kadosh.* Man's kingdoms are going to come down. God is starting in the church. He's going to dethrone them and us.

Now God also says, "Nothing shall remain the same" (Ezekiel 21:26). This is a time not only of shaking, but of abdication by shaking.

The Bible talks about a time when everything that can be shaken, will be shaken. I believe we're seeing this now. I'm just as astounded as you, but I'm not surprised how quickly God has been able to show the world its foundation. He's showing the world the sand its people have built on, and how quickly all their human endeavors have come to a screeching halt. Many church leaders are forever trying to impress with their projects and programs and entertainment. They are constantly trying to keep people excited about what they're doing.

God's shaking all that! In this time of shaking, He's telling us that nothing will remain the same. No, we're not going to return to business as usual. This is not just a light shaking. This is not a gentle nudge. This is not just a little bit of discomfort. This is a major, global shaking of humanity. Nothing will remain the same.

Do you remember the letter from David Wilkerson that I mentioned earlier? He said a shaking would take place. He predicted that judgment would fall on America; a theme which he shared in several messages and books. This appears to be taking place today.

God is shaking us. He's shaking the systems, the structures, the economy, and the political world. Everything that can be shaken is being shaken, including the church. We never thought this could happen, yet it is happening! It occurs to me that when something is being shaken, if I respond by being rigid, that shaking will break me. If I respond to that shaking by becoming flexible and humble and sensitive, then it does not break me. The shaking causes me to become less rigid. The things that I've trusted in, the places where I've found security, no longer satisfy. I see the *ruach hakodesh*, the Holy Spirit, working in His kingdom, glorifying one person, and it's not me.

I believe when this is over, there will be a remarkable change wrought by the power of the Holy Spirit, and that change will be a Third Great Awakening.

The next area He speaks to us about prophetically is exalting self. He's speaking here about man's kingdoms coming down. He's speaking about a shaking, but also a reversal. This reversal reveals that the things that have been viewed and perceived as low will suddenly be perceived as high. Conversely, the things that were perceived as high will then be seen as low.

The Bible says every mountain will be brought low, every valley raised up; every crooked way will be made straight, every rough path made smooth. But here, He's talking about the things that have been humbled now being exalted. The things that have been exalted are now being humbled. This is a picture of reversal. One change God wants to make in the church is for us to see the things we consider as being high in importance, or valuable, or a high priority, those things we must now consider insignificant.

As you take the crown off, and as you accept the fact that the shaking is going on and God is behind the shaking, He wants to do something supernatural in your life and in the life of His body, the church. That supernatural work requires a change, a different view, a different perspective. I want you to start looking at and evaluating the things that you consider to be so important, that you're so passionate about, and consider so valuable. I want you to look at something much more valuable. That is the King of kings and Lord of lords. Only He deserves the praise and recognition in your heart and in your life.

This is a reversal of value systems, a reversal of perspective, and a reversal of things we count as important. This is what the *ruach hakodesh*, the Holy Spirit, wants to do in the body of Christ. He desires to do it in you and in me.

Think about this for a moment: What's important to you? What occupies your mind and your passion? I don't want to define it for you, but I think that sometimes in the body of Christ, we've established things as being so important in our lives and our culture and our religious experience, that they're coming between us and the Lord.

How can this be possible? Can attending church, giving, singing songs, or hearing a sermon, ever come between you and the Lord? You'll never know until you see Jesus. Until you get into the presence of the Holy Spirit. Until the power of God fills you to overflowing, you'll never know.

I want you to look at these things now, because they're the things that matter. They're the eternal things. I don't want you to be sucked into a value system of the world where the church is trying to copy the world and be like the world to accommodate the world. I've met pastors who feel like they're celebrities. I had one pastor tell me, "It's a burden for me to be a celebrity." He said, "I have to have bodyguards and I can't fly on regular planes. I have to travel in private jets because I'm a celebrity."

Oh, really? I'm not. I've met with over 75 world leaders and have been in 41 war zones. I don't need bodyguards. I have angels, and I do fly commercial.

God wants to raise up the things that you may have seen as valuable, and humble you with those things. You are to bring down those things you're lifting up. I want you to notice the words: "Overthrow, overthrow, I will make it overthrown." Three times Scripture uses the word "overthrow." God is literally speaking about a complete upending.

God tells us there's a crown, but He wants us to take it off. He's saying there's a commitment to things as they are, but it's all going to change. There are things we look down upon that I want you to begin to look up at. There are things we've been looking up at that I want you to begin to look down on.

Then God will completely bring about a shaking or an upheaval. He's going to overthrow your kingdom of self, and require your abdication. There is a tremendous change God desires in the hearts and minds of His people. This change can only be revealed through the power of the Holy Spirit.

I believe with all my heart, that for the church to be a glorious church, to be a light unto the world, to plunder hell and populate heaven, the church must see this. The Lord is giving us an opportunity to abdicate our kingdom. He's giving us an opportunity to detach from the way we think things should be, an opportunity to reverse our systems. It's an opportunity to prepare for a complete shaking from the Lord that is preparing for the way of the Lord.

If our value system is the same as that of the world, we will have as many crowns on our heads as the world has. We are so attached to the things of this world that God is taking them out of the way. We are going to be very upset. We're going to be unprepared for the next move of God. However, if we embrace what God is saying and doing, if we humble ourselves and reestablish our priorities, a bright light will shine upon us, and a transformation will take place.

I've been asked by pastors over the past several months, "When is it going to get better? When is this Great Awakening going to happen?" The question is not, "When is the Great Awakening going to happen?" The question is, "When are we going to prepare ourselves for the Great Awakening?" It's coming, whether you like it or not. When it comes, you're going to see things. You're going to hear things you have never heard. You're going to do things that you have never done.

It's going to be an interrupter. God's going to interrupt your programs. He's going to interrupt with repentance. Imagine for one second, the Holy Spirit showing up in power in your church with such a roar that you can't continue with your regular program. The Holy Spirit will take over. Imagine people standing up, confessing their sins, and crying in repentance. Imagine people bowing at the front of your church, hours before the service, humbling themselves and seeking the face of God.

How can God show up with such glory and power? God can do whatever He wants. We must abdicate our throne and our rule. Let go of your control. Don't hang on to the things that you continue to hold. It's not transforming the world. He's wants you to exalt those things you look down on, and He wants you to put down those things that you've exalted. I know it's uncomfortable. It's inconvenient, but it's God's way. You need the power of the Holy Spirit. You need a fresh revelation of the cross. You need divine healing to be manifested in God's glory and supernatural repentance.

God is going to do these things, so we must get out of the way. We must humble ourselves, focusing on Him and not on our stuff. He's going to use you in a way you couldn't imagine, to transform a lost and dying world. He again says, these five very important words:

"It shall be no longer." Do you know what this means? What exists shall not exist anymore. There are some things that are going to be removed.

This is a picture to me of the Lord saying, "I want you to know some things. Not everything that you speak and say is coming from me." He's saying to you, "Not all of your worship is led by Me. Not all preaching is inspired by Me. Not all of your dreams and visions are led by Me." He's saying, "I want to have complete reign and rule of everything."

There are going to be some divine interruptions. Some things are going to change, because when the fire of the Holy Spirit falls, it transforms not only a church, but a community, a city, and a world. When things remain permanent and unchanged, then we have a problem. We attempt to control everything. With all our control and all our religious pride, we can grieve the Holy Spirit—and we don't even know we're doing it. That's the heartbreaking part of it all.

The question is: Where is our heart? What's it connected to? God is trying to shift us into a completely new perspective. He's bringing about a reversal of values. He wants us to know He's upending things on this earth. The permanency and the things that He's doing are going to usher in His glory and power and kingdom.

The COVID-19 plague has left us in a world with shuttered megachurches. We've experienced a world with closed shopping malls, a world without sports and entertainment; a world without travel, without celebrities, without weddings or funerals.

What things are going to be changed forever? God is dealing with our hearts. He's working to bring us into a new passion for Him. He desires for us to long for Him and love Him. We must return to our first love where nothing else matters. We need to take off that crown. We need to give Him all the glory and stay small in our own eyes. "Overthrow, overthrow," He says. "I will make it overthrown." For how long? He answers, ". . .until He comes whose right it is to sit on the throne."

What He's saying is to abdicate your kingdom. He's saying, get detached from the circumstances of your life, your activity. Reverse your value systems and prepare the way of the Lord. He's saying it's going to be different. He's going to manifest Himself with His glory. He's going to separate the goats from the sheep. The exalted will be denigrated. The denigrated will be exalted.

God is doing a new thing. It's all about Him. It has always been all about Him. It's God's plan for Jesus to rule and to reign. Colossians 1:15 teaches, "He is the image of the invisible God, the first-born over all creation. For by him all things were created that are on heaven and earth, visible or invisible, whether thrones or dominions or principalities or powers. All things were created through him and for him. And he is before all things, and all things consist because he is the head of the body."

Christ is the head of the body, the church. He is the beginning and the end. The purpose of my life is that in all things Jesus will have preeminence. Everything was made by Him. Everything was made through Him. Everything was made for Him. He's going to have preeminence. The question is, does He have preeminence in us now?

So much of the gospel that has been preached in our time has not been about the preeminence of Christ. It has been about the preeminence of man. God's not sharing the preeminence of His Son with us. He is establishing in this irrevocable plan and purpose that in all things—not in some things, not in most things, not in a few things, but in all things—Christ will be exalted.

Our glory is irrevocably attached to His glory. When He appears, then we will appear with Him in glory. It's never been about our glory. It's never been about our kingdom. It's never been about our preeminence. It has always been about His.

Here's what the Lord wants to say to us: "I want you to abdicate your kingdom. Stop ruling your own life. Stop trying to build your own kingdom. I want you to stop establishing your own plans. Stop creating your own ideas." We must realize that the goal of God's kingdom is to glorify Christ. When we do, all men will be lifted up to Him. When we put Him in His rightful place, when we take the crown off our heads, and let go of the things that are shaking us, we'll realize the power of the glorified Savior.

Let me ask you a question. When was the last time you had a Holy Spirit visitation in your church that was so powerful your pastor couldn't preach, the singers couldn't sing, and you couldn't even take up the offering? A time when saints were standing up, crying out in repentance, convicted by the Holy Spirit of their sins, and rushing to the altars? When was the last time you have heard a prophetic, "Thus saith the Lord," from your pastor in the pulpit, who has been with Jesus?

Many are preaching today that everything is going to be just fine. They say, "Don't worry about the coronavirus. It's the invisible enemy you need to worry about." No one's acknowledging it's the judgment of God. I'm saying it. It's the judgment of God! If you read your Bible, you'll see it's the judgment of God. When Nehemiah saw the condition of Jerusalem, the Bible says he sat down and wept and mourned and fasted and prayed before the God of heaven.

This will be a sign of the Great Awakening. There will be godly repentance in the pulpit and in the pews. Where there was luke-warm living, there will be brokenness and the fear of God. Sinners are going to be convicted of their sins in your church. Daniel cried out in Daniel 9:5, "We have sinned and committed iniquity. We have done wickedly." You can't be in the presence of a holy God and not fall on your face in repentance and anguish.

It's painful for me to say this, but a pastor I know once heard the President of the United States use God's name in vain twice in one rally in North Carolina and never opened his mouth. Instead, the pastor obsessively defended the President in every possible way on network television.

Of course, he never mentioned that the President had been using God's name in vain. He said something in his church like, "Mr. President, we love you, our church loves you, and millions of Christians love you across the country. We appreciate your strong Christian faith. We've never heard a stronger affirmation of faith than the one you gave. We're going to get through this crisis with your continued strong leadership and the power of God. We love you. We pray for you."

Yes, I'm grateful for Donald Trump. I'm thankful for all he's done for Israel and for his stand with evangelicals. But I want to tell you something. If I speak with the President and he uses God's name in vain, I will rebuke him to his face. It's not acceptable. We must speak the truth to the nation. There will never be a Great Awakening through compromise and accommodation.

You may be wondering, "What's wrong with you, Mike? You have it made; you're a number one *New York Times* bestseller. You're advising world leaders. You lead a world-famous museum. Why in the world are you saying these things?" I'll tell you why. I've come back to my first love. I've come back to the place I was when I first found Jesus. I didn't care what man thought; I only care what He thinks. I've come back to that first love, for a passion and a hunger and thirst to see a Great Awakening. I believe this with all my heart. You need to do the same, in the mighty name of Jesus!

QUESTIONS FOR DISCUSSION

✧ What would it mean for you to return to your first love of Christ? What would you need to change for this to take place?

✧ God wants you to remove your crown and acknowledge Him as your authority. What are some things you may need to lay at His feet to place Him first in your life?

✧ When we face times of plague, struggle, or judgment, we usually see it as a bad thing. However, God uses tough times to draw us closer to Him. How is He drawing you closer to Him during this time?

✧ Who do you need to challenge in their walk with God? Pray for an opportunity to share with this person and begin by preparing your own heart in humility and repentance.

A CALL TO PRAYER

"Confess your trespasses to one another, and pray for one another, that you may be healed. The effective, fervent prayer of a righteous man avails much." (James 5:16)

Prayer precedes all revivals. The call to revival is a call to prayer. Part of prayer is to confess your trespasses. The Greek word for "confess" is *homologeo*, which means "to say the same thing." You are saying what God says about sin.

When we call sin by a different name, or call rebellion by a different name, or lukewarm

Christians by a different name, we can't be heard by God. We must call things what God calls them, the way He calls them. When we do, there is a heart change and an open heaven.

Let me tell you a story of the power of prayer. Many years ago I went through a terrible eight and a half hour long operation on my neck. It was not a pleasant situation, as it included staples placed in my neck and much pain.

I returned home and tried the pain medications I had been prescribed. They made me feel depressed, so I threw them away. I called out to the Lord, "I don't really like what I'm seeing."

The Lord answered, "Then do something great for me. Something different."

I thought to myself, "What can I do? I have just come out of surgery. I'm stuck here."

The Holy Spirit said in prayer, "Go to Saudi Arabia and Iraq and preach the gospel."

"What?" I responded. "I can't go to Saudi Arabia. I don't have a visa. Billy Graham never even got a visa there."

But I was miraculously able to obtain a visa to Saudi Arabia in obedience to God's calling. The Persian Gulf War was about to break out, but I still made it to Dhahran, Saudi Arabia. I took a taxi to the Gulf Meridian Hotel in Al Khobar. The next morning, when I walked out onto the streets to preach, a crowd gathered. Do you know what can happen in Saudi Arabia for preaching the Gospel anywhere? You can have your head cut off! "Before I begin to speak," I said, "we're going to sing a song."

But there was only one problem: I'm not a singer.

However, a military policeman there who I thought had been sent to arrest me for evangelizing began to sing "His Eye Is on the Sparrow" in a deep, baritone voice. I wept! I had no idea he was a believer.

When I concluded my sermon, I returned to the hotel, wondering where to go next. While I was in prayer, the Holy Spirit whispered, "Go to the Dhahran International Hotel. Stick out your hand to the first man you see, shake his hand, and ask, 'May I go with you?'"

I had never done that before. I arrived at the hotel and stood before a revolving door. A man walked through wearing a Saudi thobe. As the Holy Spirit had directed, I stuck out my hand to shake his and asked, "May I go with you?"

He looked at me and said, "I don't know you." Of course, I was thinking the same thing about him.

"May I go with you?" I asked again.

"Yes," he answered. "Who are you?"

I told him my name.

"Where are you from?" I told him.

"You want to go with me?"

"Yes," I answered.

He said, "Then be here tomorrow morning at 6:15." I was there on time, in the dark, waiting. Suddenly, twelve jeeps drove up. I discovered later that the man was commander-in-chief of the multinational forces of Saudi Arabia.

His meeting was to give the invasion plans to the Egyptian Third Army and the Syrian high command. He thought I knew what he was doing, so he took me with him. I didn't know anything! But God did. Through the power of prayer and the Holy Spirit, I was on his helicopter.

I started sharing Jesus. He stopped me and said, "You know what you're doing? You're trying to convert me." He continued, "You know what we do for people who try to convert us? We cut their heads off on Thursdays."

I said, "My schedule is full on Thursday. I have no time for my head to be cut off."

He laughed and said, "I like you."

The helicopters landed and the awaiting soldiers all stood at attention. As my new friend inspected the troops, I walked beside him.

He took me into his tent. Here I was, a Jew in a tent with a Saudi military leader! At the end of his meeting, he whispered, "As is custom, I have to introduce you."

I added, "It's the custom, with one small correction. I want to introduce Jesus."

He told me, "If you embarrass me with these men, I will cut your head off with my own sword."

He interpreted for me while I shared the plan of salvation to the Syrian high command and the Egyptian Third Army. Afterwards, we walked out and I was wondering what to do next. The Spirit of God said, "Go to the 82nd Airborne and preach the gospel." The U.S. Force was dug in on the Kuwaiti border.

When I shared this, I was told that no one could take me there—except the French Foreign Legion. My new friend called for two additional helicopters to transport me to the location of the 82nd Airborne. There were no doors on them. As we landed, an American chaplain met us with tears in his eyes. He asked, "How did you get here?"

I answered, "God did it!"

Prayer can take you to places you've never been to do things you could never imagine, by the power of the Holy Spirit. We must widen our circle of inputs and concern. We must pray for one another, that we might be healed.

Imagine going to church, where people are crying and repenting of their sins. I can tell you, when that happens God's glory will fall upon that church. All the slick preaching and singing won't compare with the manifestation of His power. He's in the center of it all. We must start by hearing the heart of God, listening to His passion and His burdens.

One night I was at a lake with my kids and grandkids. While I was there, I had a dream about prayer. In the dream, I was by a beach and I asked, "Does anybody need prayer?" I made a big circle in the sand and instructed, "Get inside the circle." People began to step forward.

I then looked and saw the Prime Minister of Israel, Benjamin Netanyahu, and asked him, "Do you need prayer?"

He answered, "Yes."

I told him, "Get inside the circle." He complied. In the circle in my dream, I could hear my cell phone ringing. Now, I had never before heard a cell phone ring in my dreams. It kept ringing and ringing. Suddenly, I opened my eyes. My phone really was ringing and it woke me from my dream. When I answered it, it was the assistant to the Prime Minister of Israel asking, "Mr. Evans, can you hold for the Prime Minister?"

What? I had just dreamed it, and it was about three o'clock in the morning, but God did it. God works through prayer to literally change the destiny of the world.

The effectual, fervent prayer of a righteous man or woman avails much. The word "effectual" means active or energetic. It's not talking about prayer or teaching about prayer; a divine connection with God that takes place in the hearts of the people.

Most of today's millennials don't understand the meaning of the phrase "praying through." I do, because we once went to the altar to seek God. Sometimes we were there for an hour or two. We would pray until we had a breakthrough. Today, many churches don't have an altar or even a prayer room, and we wonder about the weakness of the church. The heart of man must be on fire for the glory of God through prayer to be part of this Third Great Awakening.

Religion has always aimed to put out the fire of God and manage or control it. We must enter God's presence with sincerity. Remember, the effectual fervent prayer of a righteous man avails much. The word "righteous" means one whose ways of thinking, feeling, and acting are wholly conformed to the will of God. It's not about perfection, but sincerity.

The word "sincere" means pure, clean, or sound. In other words, it is a heart that is hungry for the will of God. We must be completely hungry for the Lord. We have a position of righteousness. This is a gift to us because of the cross of Christ and the blood of the Lamb, but we must bring a condition of righteousness. Our goal must be a heart intent on living up to the position that we've been given as children of God.

I want to share another story with you. In 1980, I had a very rare neurological condition that no one could diagnose. I later found out what it was. But that neurological condition put my entire neck in spasms 24 hours a day and caused neck tremors. I visited dozens of doctors. No one could figure it out and I became depressed over it. I thought, "God, how can I minister in this pain, in this agony?"

One day I was praying. The Lord spoke to me and asked, "Son, do you see something else?" God then reminded me of Isaiah 43:18-19: "Do not remember the former things, Nor consider the things of old. Behold, I will do a new thing, Now it shall spring forth; Shall you not know it? I will even make a road in the wilderness And rivers in the desert."

God was saying to me, "Stop thinking about your condition." He wanted me to see that He was making a way in the wilderness.

I cried with joy as I answered, "Lord, this was a wonderful Scripture! Is there something else?"

He said, "Yes. Send a fax to Prime Minister Menachem Begin." It sounded strange, but I sent the fax because I was in prayer. Yes, I was in pain. My earthly body was screaming, but my spirit was fired up because of the power of the Holy Spirit. I sent the fax asking for a meeting with the Prime Minister. To my amazement, he said yes. There on the front of his response was the meeting date, the 30th of June, my birthday, in 1980.

On that day, I was sitting across from the Prime Minister when he asked, "Why did you come?" God had not told me why I should meet with him. He just said to go.

After stalling for a few minutes, I finally admitted, "Mr. Prime Minister, I don't know."

Mr. Begin laughed. "You don't know? You came, but you don't know why? Do you know anything?" The Prime Minister turned to his secretary and said, "Shake Mr. Evans' hand, you have finally met an honest man. He flies 8,000 miles to meet with the Prime Minister, and he doesn't know why."

Then Mr. Begin asked, "Mike, when God tells you why, will you come back and tell me?"

I answered, "Yes, I will."

That was on June 30th. On July 5th, I returned to his office once again.

Mr. Begin asked, "Have you learned why you have come?"

I said, "Because I met the Prime Minister of Israel yesterday."

Mr. Begin checked his calendar. "No, you're mistaken. You met me on the 30th of June."

I said, "It's not you. It's Benjamin Netanyahu." He didn't know who that was.

Begin's senior advisor was in the room and informed him, "It's Benzion's son, the brother of Yoni."

He asked me, "Do you believe God told you he is going to be the Prime Minister of Israel?"

I answered, "One hundred percent. Give him a job." He did give him a job in the government that week. For 22 years, I did not tell Benjamin Netanyahu the story I'm sharing with you now.

Isn't that amazing? Prayer can take you out of the depths of the pit and into the palace.

In James 5:16 the word "avail" means to exercise extraordinary, overcoming force in order to release the power of God. When we call things what God calls them, it widens our circle of concern. It engages our heart. It enters our innermost being with sincerity. We

---

will find that our prayer releases extraordinary, overcoming force from heaven.

I've met thousands of pastors, and I've preached at nearly 5,000 churches and events. Pastor, your job is not an easy one. There are great needs among the people in a congregation. It takes enormous courage to dare to believe God for a manifestation of the glory in your church, because you're afraid somebody's going to think you've gone too far. But the world needs to see Jesus. It needs to happen in your church, in your pulpit.

God also needs to see people truly worshiping Jesus in the pews. The only thing that will bring this is prayer, opening a mighty manifestation of God's glory. Jesus rebuked the temple worshipers and overturned their tables. Why? God's place was to be a house of prayer. They had made it a den of thieves.

Pastor, how much prayer is happening in your life? In your church? This nation is in such pain. It needs your prayers, crying out to God. This is my prayer for you today:

> Father, in the name of Jesus, may the Spirit of the Living God do what no man can do. God, send a Great Awakening. I pray you give the people and the pastors reading these words the courage to go back to their first love. Help them return to the joy they had when You first saved them and filled them with your Holy Spirit. Give

them the courage to dare to do something great for God. Help them to rescue sinners from hell and help reach people for heaven. In Jesus' name, Amen.

QUESTIONS FOR DISCUSSION

✧ In what ways do you desire to change your prayer life? What is one thing you can start today to help?

✧ James refers to the prayer of a righteous person. What does it mean to be righteous? How can you be a righteous person whose prayers are highly effective?

✧ When was a time you saw God answer prayer in a powerful way? What happened? How did this encourage you to walk more closely with the Lord?

✧ Who is God leading you to pray for in your family, work, school, or community? Intercede for this person and look for an opportunity to share God's love to meet their need.

16

A GREAT AWAKENING OR
A RUDE AWAKENING

Many people have experienced a rude awakening during the COVID-19 pandemic; they've seen the plague shut down nearly everything. It has been a rude awakening for entertainment and the sports world, for world governments, and even the worldwide economies. It has also been a rude awakening for the church and for the people who may have worshiped idols.

While it's a rude awakening, there's also going to be another Great Awakening. If you think what has happened lately is bad, this is nothing compared to the Bible's final book, Revelation. What will come upon the earth in the future will be far worse than anything we have faced recently. Yes, God is also preparing us for a Great Awakening.

This awakening is not about personalities; it's about power. God is up to something big in the church. This is not about celebrity preachers with bodyguards flying around in $30 million jets. Once, I was in Jerusalem when one of those preachers was ensconced in the presidential suite at the King David Hotel, a suite that costs $3,000 or more a night. He told me what a burden it was to be a celebrity. That attitude has nothing to do with those who will serve in God's coming Great Awakening.

It's not about a popular pastor preaching about things that he has heard from other pastors who are slick and smooth and satisfying to the flesh. It's about a man of God with the fear of God, with a, "Thus saith the Lord," message for God's people.

The First and Second Great Awakenings revealed the truth of what will happen in the Third Great Awakening. Two great awakenings have taken place in the history of America. The First Great Awakening began in the 1730s among the 13 colonies. The passionate preaching of men like Jonathan Edwards and George Whitfield spread like a fire throughout the land, calling the apathetic descendants of America's European forefathers to prayer, salvation, and repentance. Between the years of 1740 and 1742, New England's church membership doubled. Denominational barriers began to fall. The church was awakened, and society experienced changes in its views regarding women, slavery, and even government. God used this awakening to prepare America for its upcoming freedom, won against England in the Revolutionary War.

The age of accommodation had made its way across the Atlantic to the American colonies. The pride of man had replaced the humility of man's brokenness. Sincere faith in the Holy Spirit's power was mocked by the culture. What did the church do? It responded to that scorn by replacing its convictions so church services became controlled, not wanting interruptions from the Holy Ghost or manifestations. Repentance, a Holy Ghost prayer meeting, and the move of the Spirit were being replaced by calculated systems, formalities, and people-pleasing programs. It became all about people instead of all about Jesus.

I hear the theme all over the world that life is all about people. People are important, but life is not all about people. If you think that's the truth, look at Moses. Read his story, where he had millions of people wanting something other than the direction of the Lord. He had to fight with them for 40 years in the desert. Virtually everything they wanted and voted on was not of God.

Prior to the First Great Awakening, Christians were no longer caught up in the Spirit of God. They were caught up in the spirit of the world. The practice of faith had become socially comfortable, but it was spiritually empty. Prosperity and popularity were dominating the church culture in those days. Does this sound familiar? Eternal values were being replaced by temporal ones, both in the world and in the church.

Today, churches are divided. We have thousands of denominations. Virtually everybody knows somebody who has been part of a church split. What is a church split? It's the fellowship of the offended. It's usually religious flesh at war over the Lordship of Jesus Christ. The Lordship of Christ has been replaced by pride and man-pleasing performance.

I used to do a lot of hunting. One thing you discover in hunting is how animals mark their territory. Many animals will urinate on their territory so that if another animal enters their area, the intruder will be warned to stay away. In religion, there are also territorial beasts that divide believers and build walls. This is not of God.

Today, we might wonder whether Jonathan Edwards would even be invited to a church to preach a message entitled, "Sinners in the Hands of an Angry God." If he did, what would happen? If he showed up at your church service, calling your congregation "sinners" and preaching so descriptively on hell that people were crying out in anguish, what would happen?

Edwards preached that sin will send a person to hell. It was a move of the Holy Spirit. A personal relationship with God was the solution. These were religious services that were not controlled by man, but by the Holy Spirit. The bottom line was that he preached of Christ crucified, resurrected, and coming again.

It's not about the eloquence of our words or the beauty of our sanctuaries.

The apostle Paul wrote, "And I, brethren when I came to you, did not come with excellence of speech or wisdom declaring to you the testimony of God" (1 Corinthians 2:1). It's not about the breadth of our knowledge or the depth of our education. We don't need clever sermons that are copied from clever preachers. We need broken preachers who have been with Jesus.

In 1 Corinthians 2:2, Paul added, "For I determined not to know anything among you except Jesus Christ and Him crucified." Imagine someone standing up in the pulpit and declaring such a thing! It's not about our personal charisma or our polished image.

The next verse adds, "I was with you in weakness, in fear, and in much trembling" (1 Corinthians 2:3). I know many pastors throughout the world who are obsessed with pleasing people—not Jesus. They talk a good Jesus, but ultimately, they're accommodating people, board members, elders, and top donors in the church. Why is the divorce rate as high in America in the church as outside the church?

I once took about a dozen Christian leaders to meet with the Prime Minister of Israel. One of them was a businessman who served on a lot of big boards. As we were being bused around Tel Aviv, the Holy Spirit told me, "There's sin on this bus. Don't go up to Jerusalem until the house is cleaned."

I said to everyone on the bus, "There's sin on this bus. We're not going up to Jerusalem to meet with the Prime Minister until the Holy Ghost convicts you, whoever you are."

As we drove and prayed, suddenly a gentleman began to sob. His face turned bright red. Tears streamed down his face. He confessed in front of his wife and all the others on the bus that even though he was an elder in his church and served on boards of other ministries, he was involved in a homosexual lifestyle.

The Holy Spirit reveals things and helps us see things as they really are to bring genuine conviction and divine interruptions. Those interruptions can't be controlled by man. It's not about technological advances or impressive presentations. We don't need strobe lights or fog machines in the house of God. We need the cloud of the Holy Spirit.

The apostle Paul further wrote, "And my speech and my preaching were not with persuasive words of human wisdom" (1 Corinthians 2:4a). One of the most brilliant men who ever walked the earth said that his preaching was not with persuasive words of man's wisdom! He was brilliant, but he knew who his eyes were upon.

We don't need clever songs of comfort. We need songs of conviction. It's about the Spirit of God and the power of God, demonstrated by the presence of God, among the people of God: "But in demonstration of the Spirit and of power, that your faith should not be in the wisdom of men but in the power of God" (1 Corinthians 2:4b).

The First and Second Great Awakenings were based on some of the same issues in the church and the world that we're dealing with today. The ultimate results of a revival, the next Great Awakening, are going to be dramatic. They will change the spiritual climate of America the way they did in America during the first Two Great Awakenings. They will encourage individuals to come to Christ and to humble themselves, not to worship a building or a pastor. It will unify the nation. The nation will explode with spiritual growth and the fear of God.

The character of the church and the culture of America will be transformed by the Third Great Awakening. The First Great Awakening laid the foundation for one nation under God, indivisible, with liberty and justice for all. Not long after the First Great Awakening, the American Revolutionary War took place, making America the land of the free and the home of the brave.

The Second Great Awakening prepared the nation for the issues it would later face during the Civil War. We're talking about almost 200 years of revival in America because of two Great Awakenings.

The Second Great Awakening began around the year 1800, spreading quickly throughout the new frontier west of the Appalachian Mountains. Large revivals, or camp meetings, took place over the course of several days, where evangelists such as Charles Finney and Alexander Campbell preached to thousands of people at one time, urging repentance and conversion. One large meeting at

Cambridge, Kentucky, in 1802 attracted 20,000 people. A young man who witnessed the event later wrote:

> "The noise was like the roar of Niagara. The vast sea of human beings seemed to be agitated as if by a storm. I counted seven ministers all preaching at one time. Some stood on stumps, others on wagons. Some of the people were singing, others praying. Some were crying for mercy. A peculiarly strange sensation came over me. My heart beat tumultuously, my knees trembled, my lips quivered, and I felt as though I must fall to the ground."

Thousands were converted. New churches began and culture was transformed as Americans began to seek biblical wisdom for the nation's issues, including the abolition of slavery. God used this awakening as preparation for one of the nation's most difficult periods, the American Civil War, that began in 1861.

A Third Great Awakening seemed like it was going to happen in the late 1960s or 1970s, but it was stillborn because it was hijacked by Wall Street's methods of marketing that replaced prayer and fasting. Its failure to become a Third Great Awakening has a lot to do with the shallowness of the culture we're living in today. A Third Great Awakening is going to place a revived church at the center of America's culture that is alive with the presence, the power, and the purity of God, uncompromisingly declaring and proclaiming Christ crucified and the resurrection. It will be a great awakening or a rude awakening. The plague that we've experienced is the foreshadowing of what is to come.

If you want to be part of it, don't put your faith in man. Put your faith in Jesus. Get radically hungry and thirsty for Jesus just like when you first came to know Him. Go back to your first love. Become radical in repentance, radical in prayer, radical in obedience and God will choose you and anoint you like he anointed David to be part of the Third Great Awakening.

QUESTIONS FOR DISCUSSION

✧ What similarities do you see between the times of the first two Great Awakenings and our culture today?

✧ In what ways will the future be a rude awakening for those who refuse to place Christ first in their lives?

✧ How is God calling you to prepare for the next Great Awakening? What roles could you play in this future move of God?

✧ The church is critical to spiritual awakening. What can you do to become involved in a local church and encourage revival?

17

TRUE REPENTANCE

True repentance is more than the admission of guilt. When true repentance takes place, a life is transformed forever. You may not know what revival is, but I have seen it. I have held hundreds of revival meetings throughout the world. Some of them have been massive meetings. I remember one meeting in Brazil that I would call revival. In included over one million people.

What is revival? Revival is a renewed conviction of sin and repentance, followed by an intense desire to live in obedience to God. There's a Scripture that says, "He that endures to the end shall be saved" (Matthew 24:13). To endure means to remain under the Word. It's giving up our will to God in deep humility, giving Him preeminence.

Let me be clear: You can't cry out to God for cleansing if you think you're clean. I can tell you with certainty that if you're in the presence of Jesus you will recognize that you are unclean. No one is clean in the presence of Jesus. David cried out to the Lord in Psalm 51:1-2:

> "Have mercy upon me, O God, According to Your lovingkindness; According to the multitude of Your tender mercies, blot out my transgressions. Wash me thoroughly from my iniquity, And cleanse me from my sin."

He did not come as an exalted King, but as a sin-stricken man. He did not come out of a sense of ritual or duty, but out of desperation. He asked the Lord to wash him from iniquity. He admitted his rebellion. True repentance is an admission of wrong with no attempted justification.

When King Saul rebelled, he tried to excuse the sin and then explain and blame others (1 Samuel 13:11-12). In contrast, David took full responsibility for what he had done, hiding nothing.

John the Baptist rebuked the religious leaders for not bringing the fruits of repentance (Matthew 3:8). A holy God seeks the broken heart of a fallen man. It's not just about sin as an action, but about sin as a condition before God. True repentance knows that the only hope of healing for mankind is forgiveness from God. A clean heart is described in Psalm 51:7-9:

"Purge me with hyssop, and I shall be clean; Wash me, and I shall be whiter than snow. Make me hear joy and gladness, that the bones You have broken may rejoice. Hide Your face from my sins, And blot out all my iniquities."

The phrase "wash me and I shall be whiter than snow" is also noted in John 15:3 where Jesus says His followers are clean because of the word He had spoken to them. Let me give you an example of repentance: God called me to a season of repentance, but at first I wasn't sure why. I didn't know there was something wrong inside me.

Here's what happens in our lives. This is even true of pastors and other Christian leaders. A speaker will stand up before the crowds, and tell a story. It's all about the good part of the story. You tend to leave out a lot of stuff. You don't tell them about your depression, your discouragement, and the times you made mistakes. You don't tell that part. You just share about the good stuff. It's called a self-inspired narrative (S.I.N.). You've been inspired by your narrative, but it's a lie.

God dealt with me and said, "Don't you dare tell the story and leave out the pain and the agony and the mistakes you've made. Be righteous before Me. You're standing before a holy God."

I had a week of soul searching repentance, crying out before God. I cried out, "Help me Lord! Give me the courage to always tell it as it is."

A week after that, the Spirit of God told me, "I want you to go to the Congo and hold a crusade. I want you to rent the People's Palace and bring 10,000 pastors."

When I arrived in the country with my two daughters, I heard that a prayer meeting was taking place. It was evening and I thought, "That's great to see some people gathering for prayer. I should go join them."

I walked in to discover many people gathered. I was waiting in the back, getting ready to go up to the front to thank them for praying for me. Then I heard a witch doctor talking to them, saying, "He'll be here for seven days. Get stones, get close to the platform, stone him, and kill him." The witch doctor had a voodoo doll of me with big hands and feet, and he was sticking needles in it. I decided I didn't want to thank these people after all! I was definitely at the wrong meeting. I left before they saw me.

When I arrived at our outreach event the first night, the witch doctors were there. The people were throwing stones. The witch doctors held the voodoo dolls and stuck pins in them. The Lord told me to stop what I was doing and address the situation. I announced,

"Ladies and gentlemen, I need to stop. I want everyone to look at the witch doctors and their voodoo dolls. I'm telling you witch doctors to call on your god and call down his power. Let's see what your god can do."

They all started chanting and digging into their voodoo dolls. Nothing happened. I just stood there. Then I said, "Now I'm calling on my God. I declare the mighty name of Jesus." As I began to pray, I saw something I've never seen in my life. Every one of the witch doctors hit the ground and started slithering like snakes, screaming in torment at the name of Jesus. They were taking the charms off their wrists and waists that were used to worship demons. They then threw them in a pile and began lighting them on fire.

What a night! What a move of God! Because of that, the president of the country contacted me. He said, "I want you to do the evening news every night." I had never done the evening news on any medium, but every night we were the voice of the Congo. We talked about those God was healing and the lives He was changing at our events. That was the evening news!

I had trained 10,000 pastors before the crusade. It happened to be the time of the Rwanda crisis. An unspeakable number of people had been murdered. Hundreds of thousands had died during this time. But during that time we were there, we could stand in the gap. It came out of a time of great repentance. It didn't come out of great faith; it came out of a broken spirit. True repentance

---

looks beyond forgiveness to deliverance, and a heart that's changed forever.

In Psalm 51:10-11, David shared:

"Create in me a clean heart, O God,
And renew a steadfast spirit within me.
Do not cast me away from Your presence,
And do not take Your Holy Spirit from me."

A true, repentant heart is dedicated to living as a light and a testimony of hope to the world. The year of our 25th wedding anniversary, God worked in a powerful way in Cambodia. The Lord dealt with me in repentance. I was flat on my face for weeks and God spoke to me: "I want you to go to Cambodia." This was no small order. Two and a half million people had been killed in Cambodia. It's the story told in the book, *The Killing Fields.* But the Lord told me to go to a particular stadium there and preach the gospel.

The religious leaders warned me that I would be killed. I was joined by one pastor from the area as I visited the stadium. I said, "I want you to pray. Then I want you to tell me how many people you see here." There were only about 1,200 believers in the whole country at that time.

He prayed and cried, and then said, "I see 500 people."

I said, "Pray some more."

"Now I see 1,000."

We kept repeating this pattern until he said, "I see 80,000 people."

I then took him and visited with the leaders of the nation. They didn't invite me, but they were all meeting and I walked right into the middle of their meeting. I told them, "I want you to allow me to use the stadium for a crusade."

These were all Buddhists. There was not a single Christian among them as far as I knew. But I then said, "Before you answer me, every one of you hold hands and I'm going to pray."

I'll never forget what the foreign minister said. He told me I was rude and thought the Pope had sent me. But in the end, they said yes.

When I started that crusade, I was told that some people were going to attempt to kill me. On the second night of the crusade, my team said they were going to add more security. I discovered the reason they said some people were trying to kill me was because I was not honoring Buddha. Before I started the crusade that night, I said, "Everyone in this place who is Buddhist, raise your hand." Nearly everyone raised their hand.

I told them, "I know you're sick and you have needs. How many are sick and need healing?" Many hands lifted. "Okay, then let's ask Buddha to heal you."

I wanted them to see the difference between Buddha and Jesus. I said, "In the name of Buddha, be healed. Anyone who is healed, come up here and let us see." Nobody moved, but they recognized that I had respected Buddha.

Then I said, "Now we're going to respect Jesus. In the name of Jesus of Nazareth, who has sent me and whom I serve, by the power of His cross, be healed." As I said it, something happened in the back. I didn't know what to do. Two Buddhist monks in their robes were coming forward. We stood next to each other. One of the men had been born with a withered arm and his arm had just straightened!

The other monk looked at him and he said, "Bow down." These two Buddhist monks became believers in Jesus! They then stood on the platform, proclaiming the Lordship of Jesus Christ. They were healed by the power of God, yet these were men who had wanted to kill me.

That night after the service, some people really did try to kill me. The entire hotel was surrounded with soldiers with machine guns. I began to intercede. I could look out the window and see those men with their machine guns trying to break into the hotel. Then I remembered the prayer I had prayed before I traveled to Cambodia.

I recalled those words again that night as I prayed to God in my time of need: "Give me a breakthrough or bury me." The church was born that week during the crusade, but it almost cost me my life.

Repentance is powerful. The power of the Holy Spirit that moves through the heart that's repenting changes the world. But how do you recognize true repentance?

Would you write a hymn about your greatest sin and have it sung in your church like David did? The definition of repentance, the Greek word *metanoia*, means to change your mind. True repentance is not a bad feeling that deals with unresolved guilt. True repentance is a changed mind that results in a transformed life. In Psalm 24:3-6, David declared:

> "Who may ascend into the hill of the LORD?
> Or who may stand in His holy place?
> He who has clean hands and a pure heart,
> Who has not lifted up his soul to an idol,
> Nor sworn deceitfully.
> He shall receive blessing from the LORD,
> And righteousness from the God of his salvation.
> This *is* Jacob, the generation of those who seek Him,
> Who seek Your face."

King David came out of his personal prayer closet with a clean heart. Since his time, Psalm 24 has been prayed over countless kings at their coronations. This prayer has been sung in Israel when the nation was on the verge of war. It was also used in worship by the early church.

David was not born into royalty. He had been born in a remote location, growing up as a lowly shepherd in the fields of Judah. He had no idea that the black hole he lived in would become a holy hill. A penniless, ignorant boy, rejected by his father, David would become one of the most prominent figures in the history of the world. He became the most famous ancestor of Jesus Christ.

Yet David was originally unknown in Israel. His family was not in the registry of the high and mighty. He had no idea how much he would be favored because of his repentant heart.

Another important Psalm used in the early church was Psalm 118. It was also the Psalm one of the signers of Israel's Declaration of Independence told me about it in his home. He told me that on the Passover, at the time of Jesus, there was a song that the Jewish people sang, Psalm 118. Look at its words from some of its verses:

> Verse 3: Let the house of Aaron now say,
> "His mercy endures forever."

> Verse 5: I called on the LORD in distress;
> The LORD answered me and set me in a broad place.

> Verse 13: You pushed me violently, that I might fall,
> But the LORD helped me.

> Verse 18: The LORD has chastened me severely,
> But He has not given me over to death.

Verse 19: Open to me the gates of righteousness;

I will go through them,

And I will praise the LORD.

Verses 22-24: I will praise You,

For You have answered me,

And have become my salvation.

This was the LORD's doing;

It is marvelous in our eyes.

This is the day the LORD has made;

We will rejoice and be glad in it.

Jesus sang a Psalm at the Passover predicting His own crucifixion, death, and resurrection. What an astonishing revelation for you
and me! Because we're Christians, we rarely dream that we can be
the problem. Nothing is more important to God than to manifest his
Son fully and completely through the life of the believer. We pray in
faith, but don't realize that many times we're asking God to empower
our flesh.

Many Christians have tried to live the Christian life in their own
power and have failed. We haven't taken over the world; the world
has taken over the church. It's possible to pray without surrendering
to Christ, but it's impossible to surrender to Christ without praying.

The person of the Holy Spirit cannot and will not be used for an endorsement or affirmation of anyone or anything other than Christ and His ministry. This includes your church or my ministry—only Jesus. Attempting to live the Christian life in our religious flesh puts us at peace with our sins. We must humbly admit that most of our attempts to live a victorious Christian life have been in our own strength. It's the greatest obstacle to releasing God's glory.

We can accomplish more in one day of living a crucified life than in a lifetime of sincere religious intentions. The refusal to surrender complete control of our lives to Christ is a blatant declaration of war against His Lordship. When Christ resides in His rightful dwelling place on earth, the heavens are opened.

Christian religion today has become all about "me". What can I get out of it? The greatest manifestation of God's glory in the Third Great Awakening is repentance and a radical cry for intimacy with Jesus.

Let's pray that the mountains constructed of religious flesh and pursuits come down so that the valley of our lives can be filled with God's glory. Just one day of surrender to God will render more than a lifetime of religious intentions.

When self is on the throne of your life, you can be sure chaos will be the norm. No matter how religious you are, Christ has made no provision for us to live successfully in our own strength. The only provision He has made is for Him to live His life through us. By nature, we want to follow Jesus from the manger to the mansion but bypass the cross. That's why we don't hear preaching on the cross, or on sanctification, or on hell. The most important thing to God today, for which He's ready to move heaven on earth, is manifesting His Son fully and completely through our lives. Our hunger for God is the greatest indication that the person of the Holy Spirit is on the throne of our lives.

When we go after Jesus, the enemy goes after us, because we become a threat to his kingdom and his territory. I pray for you to draw so close to Jesus that when you face your plagues, instead of being proud of your accomplishments, you live with fear and trembling and a brokenness of spirit because you've seen Jesus and have been with Jesus. I pray for you as you read these words that God would give you a repentant heart and a broken spirit. I'm asking the Lord to give you a passion for Him and for His glory.

QUESTIONS FOR DISCUSSION

✧ In what ways does repentance remain important even after we have become a follower of Jesus?

✧ How can being broken before the Lord help us grow spiritually?

✧ What are some areas of life you need to confess to the Lord? Make time to pray and deal with any situations the Lord brings to your mind.

✧ After reading this book, what are some ways you believe God is calling you to serve Him and impact the lives of others?

BOOKS BY: MIKE EVANS

Israel: America's Key to Survival

Save Jerusalem

The Return

Jerusalem D.C.

Purity and Peace of Mind

Who Cries for the Hurting?

Living Fear Free

I Shall Not Want

Let My People Go

Jerusalem Betrayed

Seven Years of Shaking: A Vision

The Nuclear Bomb of Islam

Jerusalem Prophecies

Pray For Peace of Jerusalem

America's War:The Beginning of
the End

The Jerusalem Scroll

The Prayer of David

The Unanswered Prayers of Jesus

God Wrestling

The American Prophecies

Beyond Iraq: The Next Move

The Final Move beyond Iraq

Showdown with Nuclear Iran

Jimmy Carter: The Liberal Leftand
World Chaos

Atomic Iran

Cursed

Betrayed

The Light

Corrie's Reflections & Meditations

The Revolution

The Final Generation

Seven Days

The Locket

Persia: The Final Jihad

GAMECHANGER SERIES:

GameChanger

Samson Option

The Four Horsemen

THE PROTOCOLS SERIES:

The Protocols

The Candidate

Jerusalem

The History of Christian Zionism

Countdown

Ten Boom: Betsie, Promise of God

Commanded Blessing

BORN AGAIN SERIES:

Born Again: 1948

Born Again: 1967

Presidents in Prophecy

Stand with Israel

Prayer, Power and Purpose

Turning Your Pain Into Gain

Christopher Columbus, Secret Jew

Living in the F.O.G.

Finding Favor with God

Finding Favor with Man

Unleashing God's Favor

The Jewish State: The Volunteers

See You in New York

Friends of Zion:Patterson & Wingate

The Columbus Code

The Temple

Satan, You Can't Have My Country!

Satan, You Can't Have Israel!

Lights in the Darkness

The Seven Feasts of Israel

Netanyahu (a novel)

Jew-Hatred and the Church

The Visionaries

Why Was I Born?

Son, I Love You

Jerusalem DC (David's Capital)

Israel Reborn

Prayer: A Conversation with God

Shimon Peres (a novel)

Pursuing God's Presence

Ho Feng Shan (a novel)

The Good Father

The Daniel Option (a novel)

Keep the Jews Out! (a novel)

Donald Trump and Israel

A Great Awakening Is Coming!

Finding God in the Plague

TO PURCHASE, CONTACT: orders@TimeWorthyBooks.com
P. O. BOX 30000, PHOENIX, AZ 85046

MICHAEL DAVID EVANS, the #1 *New York Times* bestselling author, is an award-winning journalist/Middle East analyst. Dr. Evans has appeared on hundreds of network television and radio shows including *Good Morning America, Crossfire* and *Nightline*, and *The Rush Limbaugh Show*, and on Fox Network, *CNN World News*, NBC, ABC, and CBS. His articles have been published in the *Wall Street Journal, USA Today, Washington Times, Jerusalem Post* and newspapers worldwide. More than twenty-five million copies of his books are in print, and he is the award-winning producer of nine documentaries based on his books.

Dr. Evans is considered one of the world's leading experts on Israel and the Middle East, and is one of the most sought-after speakers on that subject. He is the chairman of the board of the ten Boom Holocaust Museum in Haarlem, Holland, and is the founder of Israel's first Christian museum located in the Friends of Zion Heritage Center in Jerusalem.

Dr. Evans has authored 105 books including: *History of Christian Zionism, Showdown with Nuclear Iran, Atomic Iran, The Next Move Beyond Iraq, The Final Move Beyond Iraq*, and *Countdown*. His body of work also includes the novels *Seven Days, GameChanger, The Samson Option, The Four Horsemen, The Locket, Born Again: 1967*, and *The Columbus Code*.

✦ ✦ ✦

Michael David Evans is available to speak or for interviews.

Contact: EVENTS@drmichaeldevans.com.

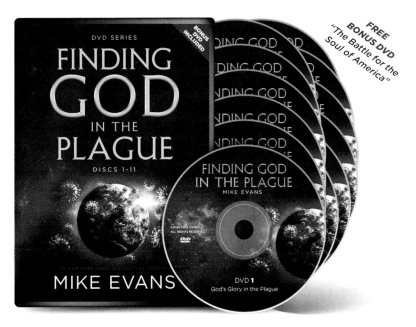